Light and Lively

Humorous American Short Stories

Mira B. Felder ■ Anna Bryks Bromberg

Longman

Light and Lively: Humorous American Short Stories

Longman, 10 Bank Street, White Plains, NY 10606-1951

Editorial Director: Joanne Dresner
Senior Acquisitions Editor: Allen Ascher
Development Editor: Randee Falk
Associate Editor: Jessica Miller
Production Editors: Thea Mohr, Karen Philippidis
Text Design: Christine Gehring-Wolf
Electronic Production Supervisor: Kim Teixeira
Composition: Reuben Kantor, Kathleen Marks
Cover design: Naomi Ganor
Cover art: George B. Kelly

Chapter opening illustrations
1 Al Lorenz
15 Tom LaPadula
25 Charles Fellows
39 Jon McIntosh
55 Don Freeman
67 David Lindroth
81 Michele Maldeau
93 Warren Lieberman
105 Jerry McDaniel
123 Terry K. Schwarz
135 Cindy Ferrara
147 Stuart Leeds
161 Hal Just
173 Terry K. Schwarz
185 Len Shalansky

Pictorial glosses by Len Shalansky and Terry K. Schwarz
Drawings on page 141 by Cindy Ferrara

Library of Congress Cataloging-in-Publication Data
Felder, Mira B.
Light and lively: Humorous American Short Stories / Mira B. Felder, Anna Bryks Bromberg.
— 2nd ed.
p. cm.
ISBN 0-201-83413-8
1. English language—Textbooks for foreign speakers. 2. Readers.
I. Bromberg, Anna Bryks. II. Title.
PE 1128.F38 1996
428.6 ' 4—dc20
96-20066
CIP

4 5 6 7 8 9 10 CRS 01 00 99 98

Contents

Preface v

Introduction vi

Unit 1 **Complaint Department**—Katherine Best 1
Verb Tenses; *Say* and *Tell;* Direct and Indirect Speech; Sentence Builder (Various Idioms); Adverbs With *Say* And *Tell;* Other Speech Verbs

Unit 2 **Are You Majoring In Detention?**—Bill Cosby 15
Articles; Imperatives and Polite Requests; Verb Tenses

Unit 3 **The Late Mr. Adams**—Steve Allen 25
Pronouns; Active and Passive Voice, Articles, Prepositions, Past Perfect

Unit 4 **My Financial Career**—Stephen Leacock 39
Spelling; Sentence Combining with *And;* Subject-Verb Agreement; Irregular Past Tense Verbs; Adjectives

Unit 5 **Old Country Advice to the American Traveler**—William Saroyan 55
Adjectives vs. Adverbs; Imperatives and *Let's;* Combining Sentences by Using Relative Pronouns; Quotation Marks; Prepositions of Time and Place

Unit 6 **This Year It's Going to Be Different**—Will Stanton 67
Present Perfect and Past Perfect; *It's* vs. *Its;* Appositives; Sentence Combining

Unit 7 **A Bird in Hand—What's It Worth?**—Elaine Hart Messmer 81
Who vs. *Whom;* Proverbs and Simple Present in Factual Statements; Comparatives

Unit 8 **You Were Perfectly Fine**—Dorothy Parker 93
Interjections; Adverbs Modifying Adjectives; Short Answers and Other Short Forms in Spoken English; Punctuation

Unit 9 **Harpist on Horseback—Hilda Cole Espy** 105
Will/Would—Future in the Past vs. Future in the Present; Future Perfect and Past Perfect; Conditionals—Real and Unreal; Infinitives and Gerunds

Unit 10 **The Awful Fate of Melpomenus Jones—Stephen Leacock** 123
Possessive Nouns; Modals; Past Continuous (vs. Simple Past)

Unit 11 **The Soft Sell—Art Buchwald** 135
Infinitives and Gerunds; Relative Clauses; Constructions with *It;* *What* Clauses for Emphasis

Unit 12 **Glove Purchase in Gibraltar—Samuel Clemens (Mark Twain)** 147
Conjunctions—*And* vs. *But;* Literary Language: Similes, Metaphors, Double Meanings; Complex Sentences; Conditional—Real

Unit 13 **What Do You Do with Your Old Coffee Grounds?—Howard Lindsay** 161
Review—Irregular Verbs; Parallelism

Unit 14 **The Romance of a Busy Broker—O. Henry** 173
Modifier Patterns; Transitional Devices; Conditional—Unreal

Unit 15 **University Days—James Thurber** 185
Part 1 185
Part 2 194
Transition Words (Coordinating and Subordinating Conjunctions, Conjunctive Adverbs); Punctuation (Commas, Semicolons); Conditional—Past Unreal

Answer Key 207

Preface

This newly revised text reflects our aim to make *Light and Lively* an interactive reader. To that end, we have introduced scanning and pre-reading questions as well as role-playing and writing activities which require the student to use varied grammatical constructs. Furthermore, we have tightened the format of the text so that all exercises are directly related to the reading selections.

We have tried to make *Light and Lively* live up to its name and to be useful as a text for intermediate students of English as a second language. The book consists of humorous readings accompanied by easy to moderately difficult exercises, making it suitable as well for community college freshmen and for students who do not speak standard English.

All the selections and exercises in the text have been extensively tested in classrooms. They are the product of many hours of teaching and experimentation both by us and by our instructor-consultants, who suggested a number of topics that would make the book more relevant to their students' needs. The exercises, which grow directly out of the stories, stress the most common communication and grammatical problems students face.

Light and Lively is organized so that it can be used both as a literary anthology and as a grammar text; for either purpose, each chapter is self-contained and requires no additional materials.

There are many people we wish to thank at Addison Wesley Longman: Joanne Dresner, Editorial Director, for first introducing us to Addison Wesley Longman and making us feel welcome; Allen Ascher, Senior Acquisitions Editor, for his encouragement and suggestions and for always being there when we needed him; Randee Falk, Developmental Editor, for giving generously of her time and expertise; Jessica Miller, Associate Editor, for being responsive to our suggestions; Thea Mohr and Karen Philippidis, Production Editors, for expertly scrutinizing every detail of the text; Victoria Denkus, Senior Marketing Associate, for being very patient, and Amy Durfy, Senior Administrative Assistant, for ensuring that the follow-up was complete. Our thanks also go to Terri Fletcher and Marina Zilberman, who typed the manuscript.

No book gets written without a great deal of help from family members. We are grateful to our parents, Harry and Fryda, and Sam and Shirley, who successfully mastered the English language without the aid of our text, and our children, Joseph, Sara, and Aaron Felder and Brian and Benjamin Bromberg, who enthusiastically commented on all aspects of *Light and Lively.* The most put-upon members of our families have been our husbands. We thank Sol Bromberg, who remained convinced that all would go well. Most importantly, we wish to thank Simon Felder, whose suggestions and editorial advice helped shape this new edition of our textbook.

We add a special note of thanks to Art Buchwald and Rosemary Thurber, who proved themselves special friends of the students for whom this book is intended by donating selections to our text.

Introduction

Light and Lively is an anthology of humorous stories and essays, most of them no more than three pages in length, that will give students a glimpse of American life and American idioms. Each section is preceded by pre-reading questions and is followed by comprehension questions (both factual and inferential), vocabulary and idiom exercises, and discussion and writing questions, in addition to a variety of grammatical exercises.

The selections are arranged in order of difficulty, with the easier, shorter pieces at the beginning of the text and the longer, more advanced ones at the end. (The last selection, "University Days," is too long to cover in one lesson and has been divided into two parts, each with its own exercises.) When two selections deal with similar topics and can be profitably used for comparison and contrast, they are placed in sequence. For example, "The Soft Sell," which is fairly easy, directly precedes the more advanced "Glove Purchase in Gibraltar" because they both examine the psychology of salesmanship.

The selections may be read in any order of the instructor's preference, since all the difficult words and expressions in every story are defined, even if they have appeared previously in another selection. Thus each chapter is a self-contained unit. Only the verb exercises are arranged in order of difficulty and build on each other as the text progresses. Therefore, if the selections are not being studied in sequence, we recommend that an instructor skip a story occasionally but not go back and forth in the text. Furthermore, the selections go from fairly simple to more complex sentence structures, so some orderly sequence is necessary. Basically, though, every chapter can be used independently to fit the instructor's preferences or students' needs.

Vocabulary

All words and phrases not easily understood from their context are defined in each selection, even though they may have appeared and have been glossed previously. If there are multiple meanings for any word or expression, we have provided all of them, with the first definition a synonym for the word as it is used in the text, so that the student can usually make a direct substitute of the definition for the word being defined.

We use three methods for defining the vocabulary and idioms: (1) New or difficult words are marked in the text by a number and are defined in the margin. (2) Idioms and phrases are indicated by an asterisk (*) and are defined in a list at the end of the story. Students should review that list before beginning to read each selection. (3) Finally, for a few other, more complex words and expressions, we have used small pictorial glosses with labels, which appear on the same or facing page.

The opening illustration for each selection aids in defining the title or in illuminating the sense of the piece. For instance, the sketch for "The Romance of a Busy Broker" shows a ticker tape, a telephone, and a typewriter—all equipment used in a brokerage house.

Exercises

The exercises, which are short and varied, are designed for maximum student participation. They not only call for standard fill-in and substitution-type answers, but will familiarize students with various American institutions and everyday situations.

Previewing the Story and Thinking about the Topic These exercises are designed to focus the student's attention on pertinent aspects of the story and to set goals for reading and interpreting the story.

Comprehension and Responding to the Story These exercises review the student's understanding of the main idea and the details of the story; inferential questions test for attention to nuances. The student must always respond in complete sentences, orally or in writing; a simple yes or no is not sufficient.

Vocabulary Since word and phrase acquisition have the greatest priority for a language student, varied vocabulary exercises appear after each selection to help reinforce the use of new words and expressions. These include fill-in, substitution, and dictionary exercises—both in and out of sentence context. Idiom exercises give students an opportunity to generate original sentences, following the example of a particular idiomatic structure.

Articles, Prepositions, and Word Forms One problem common to students of the English language is mastering the correct use of articles, prepositions, and word endings. To this end we have included many related exercises throughout the text, and we suggest that students read each sentence aloud in order to become accustomed to the correct usage.

Verbs The verb exercises deal with a wide range of skills, from knowing the simple past tense of regular verbs (something students may have already learned) to composing complete structures, such as the conditional and perfect tenses, from a model. The exercises test many different aspects of verb competence, including subject-verb agreement, regular and irregular endings, and the correct use of active and passive voice, imperatives, infinitives, and gerunds.

Sentence Structure Most selections are followed by at least one structure exercise or pattern drill. These become increasingly difficult as the text progresses and range from simple sentence combining to parallel structure, subordination, and the use of the subjunctive mood.

Other Exercises Many of the readings contain instances of particular grammatical or structural points that require elaboration and further study. These points are dealt with in exercises that treat tag endings, proverbs, direct and indirect objects, adjectives and adverbs, nationalities and languages, courses of study, the use of "will" and "would," punctuation, spelling, direct and indirect quotations, and forms of obligation.

Topics for Discussion and Writing Every group of exercises contains suggestions for discussion and writing. Although generated by the selections, they can also be used for more general assignments drawing on the students' own experiences. In many cases, an answer will require the use of a simple rhetorical device, such as simple listening, comparison-contrast, and the like, and can take the form of an oral presentation or written assignment.

Answer Key

For quick review and easy reference, an Answer Key is printed at the end of the book. The Answer Key enables the instructor to assign independent work (such as a specific grammatical exercise for review or reinforcement), knowing that the student can check his or her own answers and make corrections where necessary.

UNIT 1

Complaint Department

—KATHERINE BEST

About the Author

Katherine Best, *a magazine writer whose stories have appeared in many American publications and collections of humor, writes about the humorous difficulties encountered in everyday experiences. The following selection, taken from a collection called* The Family Book of Humor *(1958), illustrates one difficulty in dealing with a large department store.*

◆ Previewing the Story

Look at the picture, the title, and the first paragraph of the story. Answer the questions, explaining each answer.

1. Why do you think there are so many faces coming out of the telephone?
2. What do you think the story is about?
3. Do you think the person holding the telephone is having his questions answered? Explain your answer.
4. Do you think his questions are about something serious and important? Explain your answer.

◆ Thinking about the Topic

Think about and answer the following questions.

1. Do the stores in your country have a complaint department? How are complaint departments supposed to help customers?
2. Have you ever complained about a purchase you made? How did you do it? Was the process easy or difficult? Was your complaint taken care of?

Mr. Seeley shut himself in* the telephone booth. He had a small matter of business to transact[1] with T. J. Tinglefooter & Co.

[1] conduct

"Raymond 9-4000," he said to the operator.

"Good afternoon," a smooth voice greeted him. "T. J. Tinglefooter & Co."

"About three days ago," said Mr. Seeley, "my wife bought some flour at your store. . . ."

"Just a moment, sir," the smooth voice said, "I'll connect you with the grocery department."

"Good afternoon. Grocery department, T. J. Tinglefooter & Co.," said another smooth voice.

"Yes," said Mr. Seeley. "I want to tell you about some flour my wife bought. . . ."

"What is the name, please?"

"Mrs. F. D. Seeley. S-E-E-L-E-Y. 479 Crosswood Avenue, Bronxville, New York. This flour you sent, it had worms."°

small, boneless creatures

"Do you wish to register[2] a complaint?"

[2] report

"I certainly do," said Mr. Seeley. "It had worms!"

"Just a moment, sir. I'll connect you with the complaint department."*

"Good afternoon," said the complaint department, "T. J. Tinglefooter & Co."

"Is this the worm department?" asked Mr. Seeley.

"I beg your pardon."*

"I ordered some flour from you people and it was all molded or something. It had worms and I want . . ."

"Will you spell it, please?"

"Worms. W-O-R-M-S," spelled Mr. Seeley.

"And what is the nature[3] of the complaint, Mr. Worms?"

[3] type

"Worms! *That's* not *my* name! My name is Seeley. S-E-E-L-E-Y. 479 Crosswood Avenue, Bronxville, New York."

"And the initials?"

"F as in Frank, D as in David."

"Thank you. What is the street address, please?"

"I just *gave* it to you. 479 Crosswood Avenue, Bronxville, New York. You know, four as in one, two, three, four. Seven as in one, two, three, four, five, six. . . ."

"Four, seven, nyun Crosswood Avenue. Thank you. And the town, please?"

"Bronxville. *Bronxville.* And unless those worms have carried it away, it's in New York State."

"Just a moment, Mr. Seeley. You did not receive the merchandise you purchased?"

"I *did!*" shouted Mr. Seeley. "The stuff was crawly[4] with worms. It was spoiled, see? *Spoiled.* It had worms!"

"Do you wish a readjustment?"[5]

"I most certainly do!" Mr. Seeley wiped the perspiration[6] from his face. "I didn't order worms. I ordered flour."

"Just a moment, sir. I'll connect you with the readjustment department."

"Good afternoon. Readjustment department, T. J. Tinglefooter & Co." The voices were getting smoother.

"I have worms," said Mr. Seeley desolately.[7]

"I beg your pardon, sir. What department did you wish."

"I don't know. It's like this.* My wife ordered some flour and it had worms crawling all through it and I called up* to see if you . . ."

"May I have your name, please?"

"F. D. Partment."

"Your street address?"

"794 Bronxwood Avenue."

"Your town?"

"Crossville."

"Your state?"[8]

"Damned[9] bad." Mr. Seeley rarely resorted to* blasphemy.[10]

"I beg your pardon. What number did you call?"

"New York."

"Thank you. What is the nature of the complaint?"

"You see, my wife bought the loveliest sack of flour you ever saw. It was all wrapped up in pretty white paper and we could hardly wait to open it. And what do you suppose had gotten in our lovely white sack of flour? Worms, old nasty,[11] crawly worms." Mr. Seeley writhed[12] in reminiscence.[13]

"The merchandise was received in imperfect condition? Very good. What readjustment do you wish?"

[4] full; crawling

[5] correction; replacement

[6] sweat

[7] hopelessly

[8] a territorial unit of the United States; the way a person feels, someone's condition

[9] very

[10] language disrespectful of God

[11] dirty; unpleasant

[12] twisted

[13] remembrance

"I want you to send me," said Mr. Seeley wearily, "some more flour without imperfect conditions crawling all around in it."

"Just a moment, sir. I'll connect you with the order depart . . ."

Mr. Seeley left the telephone booth and went fishing. ◆

Idioms and Phrases*

shut himself in	*went in and closed the door*
complaint department	*an office set up by most large stores to deal with dissatisfied customers*
I beg your pardon	*please repeat, excuse me*
it's like this	*this is the situation*
called up	*telephoned*
resorted to	*turned to*

Post-Reading

Comprehension

1. What kind of business is T. J. Tinglefooter & Co.?
2. What was the problem that Mr. Seeley was complaining about?
3. What departments did Mr. Seeley talk to?
4. What did the employees in each department ask Mr. Seeley? How did each employee finally deal with his complaint?
5. What did Mr. Seeley want T. J. Tinglefooter & Co. to do in response to his complaint?
6. What did Mr. Seeley do in the end?

Responding to the Story

1. Why did Mr. Seeley have so much trouble explaining his problem?
2. Would Mr. Seeley have been more successful in replacing his wormy flour if he had written a letter of complaint? Why or why not?
3. Did the person in the readjustment department use the word "state" in the way that Mr. Seeley understood it? How do you know?
4. Why did Mr. Seeley give up? What do you think would have happened if he hadn't given up?
5. Why is Mr. Seeley's decision to go fishing humorous? What made him think of going fishing?
6. If you had been Mr. Seeley, would you have handled the situation differently? What would you have done?

VOCABULARY

Vocabulary Builder

Fill in the blanks with the following words.

blasphemy
resort to
register
state
readjustment
desolately
transact
nastier
reminiscence
nature
perspiration

1. Customers contact complaint departments to ____________________ their complaints and to resolve them.
2. What is the ____________________ of your complaint?
3. Usually when a customer has to ____________________ some business with the complaint department of a large store, he won't have many difficulties.
4. When people are angry, they sometimes ____________________ doing things they wouldn't normally do.
5. As his telephone call continued without results, Mr. Seeley fell into a very discouraged ____________________ and spoke, not angrily, but ____________________.
6. If a person has been exercising—or shouting—his face and body might be covered with ____________________.
7. Mr. Seeley didn't like to use ____________________ when he spoke.
8. Mr. Seeley probably had as unpleasant a ____________________ of the phone conversation as he did of the flour with worms.
9. Worms seem ____________________ when they're in flour than when they're on a fishing hook.
10. What ____________________ would you like, a new bag of flour or a store credit?

Idiom Exercise

Exercise 1

Fill in the blanks with the following idioms.

I beg your pardon
It's like this

1. "____________________," he said. "Can you tell me how to get to the complaint department?"
2. "____________________," the customer said. "You sent me the wrong size shirt."

Exercise 2

Write a sentence of your own for each of the idioms.

1. ____
2. ____

Word Forms

Fill in the blanks with the correct form of the words listed.

1. connect, connecting, connection
   a. Can you find a ________________ between worms and fishing?
   b. For better radio reception, ________________ these wires to the outdoor antenna.
   c. We missed our ________________ flight and had to wait for three more hours.
2. transact, transacting, transaction
   a. I have important business to ________________ with you.
   b. He didn't know that a simple complaint would turn into such a difficult ________________.
   c. We will not be ________________ any business on Lincoln's birthday.
3. wrap, wrapper, wrapping
   a. Joseph chose ________________ paper to ________________ the gifts he had bought.
   b. ________________ your packages carefully before mailing them.
   c. The ________________ on chewing gum keeps it fresh.

STRUCTURE

Verb Tenses

Fill in the blanks with the correct form of the verbs indicated.

EXAMPLE: Mr. Seeley didn't ______*go*______ (go) to the store to complain.

1. Maybe the next time he ________________ (have) a complaint, he ________________ (go) to the store.
2. At the end of the story, Mr. Seeley ________________ (go) fishing.

(Continued on next page)

3. Mr. Seeley ____________________ (have) very little success in transacting his business with T. J. Tinglefooter & Co.

4. It often ____________________ (take) a long time to reach the people who handle complaints.

5. While ____________________ (speak) to the readjustment department, Mr. Seeley ____________________ (realize) the situation was hopeless.

6. That day, Mr. Seeley ____________________ (speak) to four employees of T. J. Tinglefooter & Co.

7. Mr. Seeley ____________________ (leave) the phone booth in disgust.

8. When Mr. Seeley didn't answer, the employee in the ordering department probably ____________________ (think) the call had been disconnected.

9. People often ____________________ (feel) frustrated when they deal with the complaint department.

10. When you ____________________ (call) a complaint department, you ____________________ (need) to have a lot of time and patience.

11. Mr. Seeley ____________________ (give) the store employees all the information they needed.

12. Why did the employees ____________________ (give) Mr. Seeley such a hard time?

13. In the future, Mr. Seeley ____________________ (give) his business to another store.

14. This time, Mrs. Seeley ____________________ (buy) her flour from T. J. Tinglefooter & Co.; next time, the Seeleys ____________________ (buy) flour somewhere else.

Say and Tell

Fill in the blanks with the correct form of say *or* tell.

EXAMPLE: The employee in the readjustment department ____said____ that Mr. Seeley should talk to the order department.

1. Mr. Seeley ____________ his wife that he would call T. J. Tinglefooter & Co.
2. He ____________ that he would ____________ them about the worms in the flour.
3. He ____________ himself that this small transaction could be taken care of in no time.
4. Mr. Seeley ____________ the telephone operator the number he wanted to call.
5. "Good afternoon," a smooth voice ____________ to Mr. Seeley. "T. J. Tinglefooter."
6. Mr. Seeley ____________ that he had a complaint.
7. The employee listened to Mr. Seeley and then ____________ him that he needed to talk to someone else.
8. Mr. Seeley ____________ that he was going fishing.

Direct and Indirect Speech

When you use indirect speech to tell about what someone said in direct speech, you need to change verb tenses, pronouns, and certain other words. For example:

DIRECT: "I want to register a complaint," Mr. Seeley said.
INDIRECT: Mr. Seeley said that he wanted to register a complaint.

DIRECT: "What is your name?" the operator asked Mr. Seeley.
INDIRECT: The operator asked Mr. Seeley what his name was.

DIRECT: "Is this the worm department?" Mr. Seeley asked.
INDIRECT: Mr. Seeley asked whether this was the worm department.

Exercise 1

Change the following sentences from direct speech into indirect speech.

EXAMPLE: "What is your complaint?" the employee asked Mr. Seeley.
The employee asked Mr. Seeley what his complaint was.

1. "About three days ago," said Mr. Seeley, "my wife bought some flour."
2. "I'm going to connect you with the grocery department," the store employee told Mr. Seeley.

(Continued on next page)

3. "Do you wish to register a complaint?" the grocery department employee asked Mr. Seeley.
4. "What is your address?" the employee asked Mr. Seeley.
5. "I just gave you my address," Mr. Seeley told the employee.
6. "I have worms," Mr. Seeley said desolately.
7. "What readjustment do you wish?" the readjustment department employee asked Mr. Seeley.
8. "I want to be sent some flour without worms," Mr. Seeley answered.

Exercise 2

ROLE PLAY: With a partner, role-play Mr. Seeley going home that evening to Mrs. Seeley, who wants to know why he has fish and whether he has taken care of the wormy flour. Mr. Seeley tells the story, and Mrs. Seeley asks questions. Be sure to use indirect speech in telling and asking about the story.

Sentence Builder: Various Idioms

Exercise 1

Rewrite the sentences, using the patterns shown.

A. PATTERN: I'm sorry I called so late. —>
I beg your pardon. I didn't mean to call so late.

1. I'm sorry we sent you the wrong package.
2. I regret that I hurt your feelings.
3. I took your credit card by mistake.

B. PATTERN: Let's discuss my problems with the department store. —>
I want to tell you about my problems with the department store.

1. Let's talk about my complaint.
2. Let's discuss my meeting with the store manager.
3. I want to explain my problem with the complaint department.

C. PATTERN: They were looking forward to spring vacation. —>
They could hardly wait for spring vacation.

1. They were anxious to see their friends again.
2. We were eagerly expecting the delivery of our new computer.
3. I am eager to see how the new coat I bought for Tom fits him.

Exercise 2

With a partner, write a dialogue between an unhappy customer and a complaint department employee. Use all the phrases below in sentences in your dialogue. You can use the phrases in any order you want. Don't write about Mr. Seeley's problem; instead, think of some other interesting problem. When you and your partner have completed the dialogue, you can act it out for the class.

1. I beg your pardon.
2. I want to tell you about
3. it's like this
4. connect . . . with
5. register a complaint
6. call up
7. resort to
8. could / can hardly wait to / for
9. what do you suppose

Adverbs with *Say* and *Tell;* Other Speech Verbs

Fill in the blanks in the two dialogues with the most appropriate word from the following lists. Use each word only once.

Adverbs	**Verbs**
confidently	ask
politely	answer
desolately	shout
wearily	threaten
angrily	insist
firmly	

EXAMPLE: "I did!" ___*shouted*___ Mr. Seeley.

"Good afternoon. T. J. Tinglefooter & Co."

"About three days ago," said Mr. Seeley, "my wife bought some flour at your store."

(Sometime later:)

"Just a moment, Mr. Seeley. You did not receive the merchandise you purchased?"

"I did!" ________________ (1) Mr. Seeley. "The stuff was crawly with worms. It was spoiled, see? Spoiled. It had worms!"

(Continued on next page)

(Still later:)

"Good afternoon. Readjustment department, T. J. Tinglefooter & Co."

"I have worms," said Mr. Seeley ____________ (2).

(Finally:)

"The merchandise was received in imperfect condition? Very good. What readjustment do you wish?"

"I want you to send me," said Mr. Seeley ____________ (3), "some more flour without imperfect conditions crawling all around in it."

"Good afternoon, sir. May I help you?" the store employee said ____________ (4).

"I'm sure you can," the customer said ____________ (5). "When I washed this shirt for the first time, it shrank incredibly. It doesn't fit me at all now."

"Where did you buy this shirt?" the employee ____________ (6).

"I bought it here, of course," the customer ____________ (7).

"You couldn't have bought it here. We don't carry this brand."

"I'm telling you I did."

"I'm sorry, sir," the employee said ____________ (8). "This shirt is from another store."

"I bought it here," the customer ____________ (9) ____________ (10).

"Do you have the receipt?"

"No, I don't. I bought the shirt months ago."

"Then, I'm afraid I can't help you," the employee said, turning away.

"You had better help me, or I'll talk to your supervisor," the customer ____________ (11).

FOLLOW UP

Topics for Discussion

1. How do department stores in your country compare with those in the United States? Discuss, for example, items sold and services offered.
2. How would you make a complaint to a store in your country? How does the process compare to the one in the story?
3. Have you ever complained to, or tried to get information from, organizations or businesses other than department stores? What kinds of organizations or businesses were they? What was your experience?
4. Do you find store employees generally helpful or uncooperative? When you are shopping, do you like store employees to help you or do you prefer to be left on your own?
5. Have you ever had problems with a computerized bill from a store? Explain.
6. How do you feel about the automated telephone answering systems that many stores now have?
7. Many businesses now monitor, or listen in on, calls between customer service representatives and customers. Do you think this is a good idea? Why or why not?
8. Have you ever had an experience similar to Mr. Seeley's? What happened?

Topics for Writing

1. Write a short story about an experience like Mr. Seeley's that you or someone you know has had. Your story should be about one page long and can use direct or indirect speech.
2. Pretend that you are Mr. Seeley and write a letter of complaint to the manager of T. J. Tinglefooter & Co., describing your experience with the wormy flour and the store employees. Decide what you think T. J. Tinglefooter should do for you to make up for the bad experience, and include this in the letter as well.
3. Write a letter of complaint to a manager about a problem you have had with his or her store.
4. Write a different ending for "Complaint Department" in which Mr. Seeley stays in the telephone booth. Omit the last sentence of the actual story, and start with the sentences before ("Just a moment, sir. I'll connect you with the order department."). Make your ending as long, and as funny, as you want.

UNIT 2

Are You Majoring in Detention?

—BILL COSBY

About the Author

Bill Cosby *(1937–), a well-known comedian and movie and television star, is also the author of more than half a dozen humorous books, most of them autobiographical. He was born in Philadelphia. He attended Temple University and the University of Massachusetts, where he earned a doctorate in education at the age of 40 when he was already a famous performer. This selection is taken from his book* Childhood *(1992), in which he discusses his experiences as a student as well as his later experiences as a father of students.*

◆ Previewing the Story

Look at the picture, the title, and the first paragraph of the story. Answer the questions, explaining each answer.

1. What is the relationship between the girl and the man?
2. What do you think they are discussing? What is the girl trying to hide?
3. How does the girl feel?
4. What do you think the story is about?

◆ Thinking about the Topic

Think about and answer the following questions.

1. What is the system of grading in the schools in your country?
2. Have you taken true-false tests and essay tests? Which kind of test do you think is more difficult?
3. How involved do you think parents should be in their children's schoolwork?
4. What did your teachers do when someone didn't act appropriately in class? Did the teachers use detention as a punishment?

The American school has changed dramatically[1] since those lively days of my boyhood, and the change seems to have made it a much less eventful[2] place. In fact, nothing ever happens there now. I know this remarkable[3] truth because every day that I met one of my children after school, I said, "How was school today?"

And the child would reply, "Okay, I guess."[4]

"You guess? Don't you remember? It wasn't that long ago."

"Okay, I guess."

"You're still guessing. You don't have to study for these questions, you know."

"What questions?"

"Look, you just spent six hours in school. Didn't *anything* happen there today?"

"Like what?"

"Oh . . . I don't know. The arrival of locusts?"[5]

"What're they?"

"You remember the plagues[6] that hit Egypt?"

"Who's Egypt?"

"All right, just tell me this and then your lawyer can release[7] you: Did everything go well in all your classes?"

"It was okay."

"And you're not guessing, right?"

I have never met a father or mother who got anything other than true-false answers to after-school questions. There is probably no way to get an essay answer, even if you asked the two questions most relevant[8] to your child's life at school:

—Did you find any of the jackets, shoes, books, and underpants you've lost?

—Did you make any new friends in detention?[9]

* * *

[1] very much

[2] full of important happenings

[3] unusual

[4] form an opinion without many facts

[5] an insect that destroys plants

[6] mentioned in the Bible, something that causes terrible trouble

[7] free

[8] related to

[9] a punishment in which misbehaving students are kept after school

The best that a parent can do today is be semi-involved[10] in the schoolwork of a child.

"Sign this test, Dad," said my youngest daughter one evening, her left hand casually[11] draped[12] across the top two inches of the front page.

"May I see the mark[13] first?" I replied.

"It's not important. You and Mom always say it's learning, not marks, that counts."

"Right, and I'd like to learn about your mark."

"Trust me,* I got one."

"I appreciate your sharing[14] that with me. And now I'd like to see it."

"You mean you'll only sign for a high one? I thought you were an equal-opportunity[15] father."

"Is it lower than a D?"[16]

"Dad, you have to remember that a mark is merely[17] the teacher's opinion."

"Is it lower than an F?[18] Have you gotten the world's first G?"

"The thing is, she should have marked this test on a curve."*

"I don't care if she should have marked it on a *ramp.*[19] If you don't move your hand, I don't move mine."

Slowly, she lifted her hand to reveal[20] a bright red D.

"But this doesn't mean what you think," she said.

"Oh," I said, "it stands for* delightful?"[21]

"No, it's a *high* D."

"Good. You'll have no trouble getting into a barber college. Tell me, did you study for this test?"

"Oh, absolutely.[22] I really did."

"Then how could you have gotten a D?"

"Because I studied the wrong things. But Dad, isn't it better to study the wrong things than not to study the right ones?"

And one of the wrong things to study is a child, for only a child can make you think that F is her teacher's initial.[23] ◆

[10] partly included
[11] informally, naturally
[12] hung
[13] letter or number that shows how well a student did
[14] letting (me) know about, using together
[15] treating all the same (usually used in job-hiring situations)
[16] lowest passing grade
[17] only, nothing more than
[18] failing grade
[19] a man-made slope that connects two levels
[20] show plainly
[21] greatly pleasing
[22] definitely
[23] first letter of a name

IDIOMS AND PHRASES*

trust me	*believe me*
marked on a curve	*graded a test by comparing it with other students' marks*
stand for	*mean*

POST-READING

Comprehension

1. What does the author think of the present American school system?
2. What example does the author give of being "semi-involved" in his child's schoolwork?
3. Why is the child hiding her grade from her father?
4. Why must a parent sign the test?
5. The daughter argues that her grade isn't so bad. What reason does she give for this?
6. What excuse does she make for her bad grade?

Responding to the Story

1. What does the author mean when he says that parents get true-false answers, instead of essay answers, to their questions? Why do you think this happens?
2. Do you think it is important for parents to be involved in their children's schoolwork? Why or why not?
3. Do you think this father could do anything to become more involved with his children's schoolwork? If so, what?
4. Is the father unhappy about his children's education? If so, what exactly does he seem to be unhappy about?
5. Judging from the story, what kind of relationship do you think the author has with his children?

Vocabulary

Vocabulary Builder

Match each word in the first column with the word or phrase in the second column that is closest to it in meaning.

1. dramatically	a. hung
2. merely	b. show plainly
3. relevant	c. grade
4. remarkable	d. full of important happenings
5. draped	e. informally
6. mark (*n.*)	f. greatly pleasing
7. reveal	g. only
8. eventful	h. very much
9. delightful	i. related to
10. casually	j. unusual

Word Forms

Fill in the blanks with the correct form of the words listed.

1. arrival, arrived, arriving
   a. Dad's ____________________ in class made the teacher nervous.
   b. I ____________________ home in time to study for the test.
   c. Because my plane was ____________________ early, Dad could not meet me.
2. event, eventful, uneventfully
   a. School is no longer ____________________.
   b. When I was young, there was an exciting ____________________ each day.
   c. My child seems to find that the entire school year passes ____________________.
3. detain, detention, detained
   a. If you're in a hurry, please don't let me ____________________ you.
   b. The students were ____________________ for questioning after someone was hurt.
   c. She has to stay for ____________________ because she was noisy in class.

4. delight, delightful, delighted
   a. He didn't seem ____________________ when he saw the test paper.
   b. I guess there is nothing ____________________ about a D.
   c. He's more likely to express ____________________ at an A.
5. appreciate, appreciation, appreciative
   a. I ____________________ your sharing that with me.
   b. She was ____________________ of the interest her father took in her schoolwork.
   c. He accepted the scholarship with great ____________________.

STRUCTURE

Articles

Fill in the blanks with the article a, an, *or* the.

EXAMPLE: May I see ______*the*______ mark first?

Well, it took ______(1)______ hour before my daughter showed me her mark on her test, and it took me ______(2)______ half-hour to decide whether to sign it.

Then I asked to see ______(3)______ composition that she had written. On ______(4)______ top of ______(5)______ composition was ______(6)______ bright red D. I asked her if "D" was ______(7)______ title of ______(8)______ composition. ______(9)______ sweet smile spread across her face, and she said, "Yes, Daddy. How did you know? 'D' stands for 'delightful,' and that's what my teacher thought of my composition."

Verb Tenses

Fill in the blanks with the correct form of the verbs indicated.

Example: Children today often ___*don't communicate*___ (not communicate) with their parents about school.

1. The American school __________ (change) dramatically since I was a boy.
2. Nothing ever __________ (happen) there now.
3. Last week I __________ (meet) one of my children after school.
4. "You __________ (spend) six hours in school today," I said to my daughter.
5. In my many years as a parent, I __________ never __________ (meet) a parent who got anything but "yes" and "no" answers to his or her questions.
6. After having argued with me, she finally __________ (lift) her hand to reveal a bright red D.
7. I __________ (get) a D on the test last week because I __________ (study) the wrong things.
8. If you __________ (study), you will be successful.
9. I __________ (not move) my hand until you move your hand.
10. __________ (get) yourself a tutor before you __________ (fail) another test.

Sentence Builder: Imperatives and Polite Requests

In the story the daughter uses an imperative: "Sign this test, Dad." The father replies with a polite request: "May I see the mark first?" Rewrite the sentences below by changing the imperatives into polite requests and changing the polite requests into imperatives.

A. PATTERN: May I see the mark first? —>
Show me the mark first.

1. I'd like to see it.
2. Could you tell me what you did in school?
3. Can you try to do better on the next test?
4. Could you explain this poor grade to me?
5. Could you tell me what a leaf looks like?

B. PATTERN: Sign this test, Dad. —>
Could you sign this test, Dad? (other answers are possible)

1. Trust me, Dad.
2. Move your hand.
3. Turn off the TV.
4. Do your homework with the TV off.
5. Show me your homework.

DISCUSSION: In the situation in the story, the daughter uses an imperative and the father uses a polite request. Does this surprise you? When are imperatives usually used in English (in what situations and with what people)? When are polite requests usually used? Are there times when you are not sure which to use? In a group, discuss the use of imperatives and polite requests.

FOLLOW UP

Topics for Discussion

1. What are some of your personal experiences regarding your parents' interest in your schoolwork? Explain.
2. Should tests sometimes be marked on a curve? If so, under what circumstances? Explain your answers.
3. What do you think is the best way to measure a student's progress in school? Explain.
4. In what ways, if any, are students today different from students in the past?

(Continued on next page)

5. Lack of parental involvement in schoolwork is a common problem today. What do you think are some other problems students face?
6. ***Role Play:*** With a partner, role-play a teenager who has gotten bad marks on a report card and must tell his/her parents, who are expecting a good report card. Both the parents and the teenager should use as many *yes-no* questions as possible.

Topics for Writing

1. Write an essay about your relationship with one of your parents and/or children.
2. Describe an incident when your parents either embarrassed or helped you in school.
3. Write a letter advising one of your younger friends or siblings what to study in school and how to study effectively.
4. The author writes about two encounters with his children. How do the children see these encounters? Choose one of the encounters and pretend that you are the child involved. Write about the encounter from your perspective.

UNIT 3

The Late Mr. Adams

—STEVE ALLEN

About the Author

__Steve Allen__ (1921–), a well-known comedian and television performer, is also the author of more than a dozen books and some three thousand songs. Born in New York City into a family of entertainers, he lived with various aunts and attended eighteen schools before his graduation from high school. He writes poetry, novels, and nonfiction and can play almost any musical instrument. Allen has written of his many talents in his autobiography, Mark It and Strike It *(1960). The following selection is taken from a collection of his stories,* Fourteen for Tonight *(1955).*

◆ Previewing the Story

Look at the picture, the title, and the first paragraph of the story. Answer the questions, explaining each answer.

1. What is the connection between the picture and the title?
2. Why do you think the man in the picture is smiling? What kind of attitude might he have toward lateness?
3. The title has two meanings, based on two meanings of the word *late*. Do you know what these two meanings of *late* are?
4. Why is the person in the picture lying down?

◆ Thinking about the Topic

1. Have you known anyone who is always late? How have you and others reacted to this person's lateness?
2. In your culture, is being late considered bad manners? How do people generally react to lateness?

Mr. Adams, to get right to the point, was born late. The doctor had solemnly[1] wiped his spectacles,[2] pursed[3] his lips, made the sort of face all doctors are supposed to make after wiping their spectacles and pursing their lips, and announced that George Adams would be born on August 23.

On August 22 his mother felt pains and retired[4] to await George's arrival. On August 29 the doctor suggested light housework and a change of diet, reexamined his calculations, and stated with assured[5] finality that George would be born within two days. George was born seven days later.

Till the day he died George loved to tell the story of his long-delayed arrival, and I suppose psychologists might suggest that his lifelong addiction[6] to tardiness[7] was a subconscious means of recapturing the glory, such as it was, that was his on the occasion of his birth.

They say that the worst thief in the world is an honest man 99 percent of the time. They say that except on certain days of the week Hitler wasn't an altogether unlikable sort of chap.[8] They say that all beautiful women have their unattractive moments, that saints sometimes sin, and that the New York Yankees don't always defeat their opponents from Philadelphia.

They say that nobody runs entirely true to type.* But they are wrong. George Adams was late coming into this world, he was late being weaned,[9] he was late learning to speak, he was late for school habitually from the first day he attended kindergarten, and with very rare exceptions he was late for every blessed[10] appointment of any importance that was ever included in his busy schedule.

His other vices,[11] fortunately, were few and of relative unimportance, and his virtues[12] were many. He always managed somehow to discharge[13] his educational responsibilities with ease, and when he graduated from the state university he was in the upper tenth of his class.

He was, needless to say,* tardy in arriving at the graduation ceremony, but his dean[14] was in no way surprised by this circumstance, and George's diploma was handed to him privately after the

[1] with dignity, seriously
[2] eyeglasses
[3] pulled tightly together
[4] went to bed
[5] certain
[6] bad habit that is hard to change
[7] lateness
[8] man
[9] changed from mother's milk to other food
[10] (slang) damned
[11] bad qualities
[12] good qualities
[13] perform
[14] administrative officer of a university

speechmaking and singing had ended and the janitors[15] were beginning to fold up the auditorium chairs and put them away.

George's father soon thereafter made an opening at his plant[16] and George filled it neatly. His father, with great wisdom, instructed George's secretary to lie deliberately[17] to George regarding the times of all especially important business appointments, so that when George had to meet a business associate[18] for lunch at one o'clock he usually was given the impression that the engagement was set for twelve-thirty, and so when he sauntered[19] onto the scene at something like twelve-fifty-four there was really no harm done.

George made a great many friends as a junior executive[20] and in no time was promoted and given a substantial[21] increase in income. While not handsome he was more than slightly attractive, women found him amusing, and so one day when he announced that he was engaged to be married the news was not entirely unexpected.

His father, fortunately, had the presence of mind* to warn George's bride that her husband-to-be might arrive a few minutes late for the wedding service, so although she was visibly annoyed[22] by this eventuality[23] when it came to pass,* she was not driven to tears* and there was really no scene[24] at all. Besides, George had the best of excuses: he had stopped to have his car washed and to make a long-distance telephone call to a hotel in New York to make absolutely certain the honeymoon suite* had been reserved.

George usually had a good excuse, as a matter of fact.* He wasn't late on purpose; his intentions were the best in the world. It was just that most of the time, what with one thing and another coming up at the last minute, he never quite seemed to get anywhere as early as he wanted to.

In later years George came to be a prominent[25] citizen of the town, and there was even talk one year of running[26] him for mayor. He declined this honor, however, and continued to devote himself to private endeavor. After his father died he assumed[27] the presidency of the plant and rendered the company distinguished service.* His marriage withal[28] was a happy one and his children, four in number, were a fine-looking group at the funeral not long ago.

Everyone said it was one of the nicest funerals in recent years, and though George's family was heartbroken, you could see they were still

[15] people who clean and make repairs in buildings

[16] factory

[17] on purpose

[18] fellow worker

[19] strolled or walked slowly

[20] business manager, administrator

[21] large

[22] made somewhat angry

[23] possibility

[24] public display of strong emotion

[25] important

[26] suggesting (for public office)

[27] took on, took over

[28] in addition

able to feel a glow of pride as they looked over the crowd that packed into the church to pay its respects and hear the funeral oration.

I suppose there must have been many in the crowd who were aware that, in dying, George Adams was early for almost the first time in his life. His physician, who had detected a serious heart condition, had given him two years to live, at the outside,* and the good doctor was as shocked[29] as the townspeople when, three weeks after his examination, diagnosis, and prediction, his patient quietly passed away* in his sleep.

The caravan of sleek,[30] black limousines winding[31] to the cemetery was imposing, indeed, and the casual passerby must have concluded that a very important personage was being laid to rest.*

One minor mishap[32] interrupted the smooth flow of events, incidentally, at what was, to all practical purposes, the very last minute. The hearse[33] that carried George's coffin must have run over a nail in the road, for one of its tires went suddenly quite flat and the driver and his assistant pulled over to the roadside to replace it with a spare. After a hasty[34] conference it was decided that all the other cars should proceed, as planned, directly to the burial ground. This they did and the mourners, stepping out of the limousines sedately,[35] clustered[36] around the Adams plot and stood conversing in whispers, waiting for George.

He arrived only 23 minutes late. ◆

[29] greatly surprised

[30] smooth and shiny

[31] traveling a road with turns and curves

[32] accident

[33] funeral car

[34] quick

[35] calmly, seriously

[36] gathered in groups

Idioms and Phrases*

runs entirely true to type	*always acts as expected*
needless to say	*unnecessary to say (not surprisingly)*
presence of mind	*awareness, common sense*
came to pass	*happened*
driven to tears	*caused to cry*
honeymoon suite	*deluxe hotel room for newly married people*
as a matter of fact	*actually*
rendered the company distinguished service	*benefited or helped it*
at the outside	*at the most*
passed away	*died*
laid to rest	*buried*

POST-READING

Understanding the Story

1. What advice did the doctor give George's mother? Why did he give her this advice?
2. What kind of student was George?
3. How did George get his diploma?
4. Why was George late for his wedding? How did his bride feel about his lateness?
5. Where did George get a job? What position did he hold?
6. How did George's father make sure George was on time for his appointments?
7. George was early only once in his life. When was this?
8. How late was George for his funeral? Why was he late?

Responding to the Story

1. How did the people George knew react to his lateness? Why do you think they reacted this way? How do you think you would have reacted to it?
2. What good qualities did George have to make up for his lateness?
3. Do you think George could have been taught to be on time? How do you think he could have been taught this? Explain your answer.
4. Would you say that George was an unusual person or an ordinary person? Explain your answer.
5. How do you think George would have felt about his funeral? How was his funeral the same as his life?

VOCABULARY

Vocabulary Builder

Replace the underlined word in each sentence with the correct synonym from the list.

important	lateness
quick	rather large
seriously	university administrator
possibility	business administrator

came together	shiny
calmly	took on
cleaning/repair people	on purpose
accident	fellow worker
went to bed	strolled
bad habits and qualities	good qualities

1. The doctor solemnly wiped his eyeglasses.
2. On August 22, George's mother retired to await his arrival.
3. George was known for his tardiness.
4. His other vices, fortunately, were few and of relative unimportance.
5. George arrived for his graduation when the janitors were putting away the chairs.
6. The dean handed George his diploma after the graduation ceremony.
7. At first, George worked in his father's company as a junior executive.
8. His father instructed George's secretary to lie deliberately to George regarding the time of all important business appointments.
9. When George had to meet a business associate for lunch at one o'clock, he usually was given the impression that the engagement was set for twelve-thirty.
10. When he sauntered onto the scene at twelve-fifty-four, there was really no harm done.
11. George soon received both a promotion and a substantial increase in salary.
12. Although his bride was visibly annoyed by the eventuality, when it came to pass, she was not driven to tears.
13. His virtues were many.
14. After his father died, he assumed the presidency of the plant.
15. In later years, George came to be a prominent citizen of the town.
16. There were many sleek limousines driving to the funeral.
17. There was a mishap with the hearse.
18. After a hasty conference, the driver and his assistant decided that the other cars should go to the cemetery.
19. The mourners stepped sedately out of their cars.
20. The mourners clustered around the Adams plot.

Idiom Exercise

Write a sentence of your own using each idiom.

EXAMPLE: He had enough *presence of mind* to warn her that George might be late.

She had enough ___presence of mind___ to leave the building when the fire started.

1. George is late today, and, *as a matter of fact,* he is always late.
   ________________ and, as a matter of fact, ________________.
2. George *ran true to type* because he was late even for his own funeral.
   ________________ ran true to type because ________________.
3. He was given two years to live, *at the outside.*
   ________________, at the outside.
4. *Needless to say,* he kept his bride waiting.
   Needless to say, ________________.
5. Three weeks after his medical examination, George *passed away.*
   ________________ passed away.

STRUCTURE

Pronouns

Exercise 1

Fill in the blanks with the correct pronoun from the list, and give the reason for your choice. Each pronoun may be used more than once or not at all.

he	him	his	she	her
it	its	they	them	their
theirs	himself	themselves	anybody	nobody
another	anything	who	whom	

EXAMPLE: George was late for every appointment in ___his___ busy schedule.

1. Until the day he died, George loved to tell the story of ________ long-delayed arrival; psychologists might suggest that ________ lifelong addiction to tardiness was a subconscious means of recapturing the glory, such as ________ was, that was ________ on the occasion of ________ birth.

2. __________________ say that all beautiful women have ____________ unattractive moments and that the New York Yankees don't always defeat __________________ opponents from Philadelphia.
3. __________________ say that __________________ runs entirely true to type, but George did.
4. George's diploma was handed to __________________ privately when the janitors were beginning to fold up the auditorium chairs and put __________________ away.
5. Although George was not handsome, __________________ was more than slightly attractive, and women found __________________ amusing.
6. __________________ father had the presence of mind to warn George's bride that __________________ husband-to-be might arrive a few minutes late, so although __________________ was visibly annoyed by this eventuality, when __________________ came to pass, __________________ was not driven to tears.
7. After a few years, George was promoted by__________________ father.
8. George and __________________ wife had a happy marriage; there were no problems between George and __________________.
9. With one thing and __________________ coming up at the last minute, George never was as early as __________________ intended to be.
10. It was __________________ secretary __________________ always made sure George was on time for appointments.
11. When George was asked to run for public office, __________________ declined the honor and continued to devote __________________ to private endeavor.
12. The family felt a glow of pride as __________________ looked over the crowd that packed into the church to pay ________________ respects.
13. George left __________________ wife and four children when __________________ died.
14. George's children had loved __________________, and at the funeral people could see the great sadness felt by __________________ and __________________ mother.
15. One of the tires of the hearse went flat, and the driver pulled over to replace __________________ with a spare.

Exercise 2

In pairs or in small groups, write a humorous story in several paragraphs, using as many of the pronouns from the previous exercise as possible. Read your story to the class.

Active and Passive Voice

A verb is said to be **passive**—and a sentence to be in the **passive voice**—when the subject receives or undergoes the action. For example, in *George's diploma was handed to him by the dean*, *was handed* is a passive verb and the sentence is in the passive voice, as the subject, *George's diploma,* receives the action.

A verb is said to be **active**—and a sentence to be in the **active voice**—when the subject performs the action. For example, in *The dean handed George his diploma*, *handed* is an active verb and the sentence is in the active voice, as the subject, *the dean,* performs the action.

Change the following sentences from the passive to the active voice.

EXAMPLE: The diploma was handed to him by the dean.
The dean handed him the diploma.

1. He was given the impression by his secretary that the engagement was for twelve-thirty.
2. Actually, the engagement was set by the secretary for one o'clock.
3. The honeymoon suite had been reserved by George.
4. George's car was washed by the garage attendant before the wedding.
5. She was warned of his lateness by his father.
6. George was promoted by his father in no time.
7. George was also given an increase by his father.
8. When the old man died, the presidency of the plant was assumed by George.
9. The story of his late arrival was often told by George.
10. The flat tire was replaced by the driver and his assistant.

Articles

Fill in the blanks with the articles a, an, *or* the; *write* Ø *if no article is needed.*

EXAMPLE: ____*The*____ doctor suggested light housework and ____*a*____ change of diet.

1. On August 22, his mother felt ________ pains and retired to await George's arrival.
2. Till ________ day he died, George loved to tell ________ story of his long-delayed arrival.
3. Psychologists might suggest that his lifelong addiction to ________ tardiness was ________ subconscious means of recapturing ________ glory that was his on ________ day of his birth.
4. They say that ________ worst thief in ________ world is ________ honest man 99 percent of ________ time.

5. He was in ________________ top 10 percent of his class.
6. He was tardy in arriving at ________________ graduation ceremony.
7. ________________ school's janitors were beginning to fold up ________________ auditorium chairs.
8. George's father made ________________ opening at his plant.
9. When George had to meet ________________ associate for lunch at one o'clock, he was told ________________ lunch was at twelve-thirty.
10. George made ________________ great many friends as ________________ junior executive.
11. ________________ news that he was engaged to be married was not unexpected.
12. He had stopped to make ________________ long-distance telephone call to ________________ hotel in New York.
13. George usually had ________________ good excuse.
14. George's marriage was ________________ happy one.
15. His children were ________________ fine-looking group.
16. He assumed ________________ presidency of ________________ plant when his father died.
17. It was one of ________________ nicest funerals in recent years.
18. ________________ caravan of ________________ black limousines winding to ________________ cemetery was imposing.

Prepositions

Exercise 1

Fill in each blank with an appropriate preposition from the list. The prepositions can be used more than once.

after	around	for	in	into
of	on	over	to	with

Suppose George had fallen in love ________________ (1) a woman who was less understanding ________________ (2) his lateness than his bride-to-be. Do you think she would have married him anyway because ________________ (3) his other good qualities, or would his addiction ________________ (4) being late have ended the romance?

Do you think he would have changed if she had said that she would not marry him unless he learned to be ________________ (5) time? If he had changed, how long would he have continued to be ________________ (6) time after the wedding?

(Continued on next page)

George died ____________ (7) his sleep only three weeks ____________ (8) the doctor had told him he would likely live ____________ (9) two years. A large crowd ____________ (10) people packed ____________ (11) the church. Then many ____________ (12) them piled ____________ (13) limousines to go ____________ (14) the funeral. But because the hearse ____________ (15) George's coffin ran ____________ (16) a nail, the funeral was delayed. The mourners stood ____________ (17) the grave, waiting ____________ (18) George. ____________ (19) death, as ____________ (20) life, George was late.

Exercise 2

ROLE PLAY: In pairs or small groups, write a dialogue between someone who is absentminded and a husband, wife, or friend of that person. The absentminded person forgets everything (where he or she has put things, when he or she must be somewhere, and so on) and won't admit it. Make the dialogue humorous, and use as many prepositions as possible. Role-play the dialogue for the class.

Past Perfect Tense

The **past perfect tense** expresses a past time that comes before another past time. Use the past perfect with the simple past tense to show which of two events in the past happened first. The event in the past perfect happened before the event in the simple past tense.

The past perfect tense is formed by using *had* (the past form of the auxiliary verb *have*) plus the past participle of another verb.

Use one past perfect verb and one simple past tense verb to complete each of the following sentences.

EXAMPLE: George ___*loved*___ (love) to tell people that he ___*had arrived*___ (arrive) late.

1. George ____________ (be) born after his mother ____________ (do) some light housework.

2. After he ____________ (wipe) his spectacles, the doctor ____________ (announce) that George would be born on August 23.

3. Before George ____________ at his graduation, the janitors
(arrive)
____________ the chairs.
(fold)

4. George ____________ his diploma after the speechmaking
(receive)
and singing ____________.
(end)

5. George's father ____________ an opening for him at his
(make)
plant after George ____________ school.
(finish)

6. George ____________ on time because his secretary
(be)
____________ him to be there an hour earlier.
(instruct)

7. By the time he ____________ a junior executive, he
(become)
____________ a substantial increase in income.
(receive)

8. Even after George ____________ a senior executive, he
(become)
____________ to make many friends.
(continue)

9. George ____________ his wife that he ____________
(tell) (stop)
to have his car washed before coming to the wedding ceremony.

10. After his physician ____________ a serious heart condition,
(detect)
he ____________ George two years to live, at the outside.
(give)

Follow Up

Topics for Discussion

1. Is constant lateness just a bad habit, or are there psychological reasons for it?
2. What are your attitudes toward lateness? Do you think being on time is extremely important or not that important? Do you think lateness is more acceptable in some circumstances than in others? When it comes to being on time, is your behavior consistent with your attitudes?
3. Compare the importance of being on time in your culture with its importance in the United States. Consider various specific circumstances—for example, being on time to school, to work, to social events.

(Continued on next page)

4. Suppose George had not been able to go into his father's business. Do you think he would still have been able to get away with being late? Why or why not?
5. ***Role Play:*** Pretend you are George's father. How would you instruct George's secretary to handle George's business appointments so that he will be on time? Try acting out the scene with a classmate who will take the role of George's secretary.

Topics for Writing

1. What do you think is the greatest virtue? the greatest vice? Write an essay of several paragraphs on the greatest virtue or the greatest vice. Be sure to give supporting reasons and examples.
2. "The Late Mr. Adams" is the story of a man who has the vice of lateness. Write a one-page story about a person who has some other vice (or virtue). What is this person's vice (or virtue)? How does it affect his or her life?
3. Have you ever known someone who runs almost entirely true to type? Write a brief essay about this person. What was the type (i.e., the characteristic) that he or she ran true to? Was there an occasion on which he or she didn't run true to type? What happened on this occasion?
4. The author provides just an overview of George's life. Write a short story giving details about some event in, or some aspect of, George's life. Try writing the story from the point of view of someone who knew him—for example, his secretary, his mother or father, his wife, one of his children, or a friend.
5. Pretend that you are a newspaper reporter assigned to cover George's funeral. Write an article that summarizes George's life and describes his funeral. Use information from the story and, if you want, make up some information as well.

UNIT 4

My Financial Career

—STEPHEN LEACOCK

STEPHEN LEACOCK *(1869–1944) was born in England but moved with his parents to Canada, where he remained for the rest of his life—except for a brief period during which he attended the University of Chicago and received a Ph.D. in economics and political science. A distinguished scholar, he became chairman of the Department of Economics and Political Science at McGill University in Montreal. Despite his scholarly achievements, he is best known for his satirical and humorous writing. Leacock wrote over three hundred essays, articles, and humorous pieces during his lifetime. In the preface to* Sunshine Sketches of a Little Town *(1912) he remarked: "Personally, I would sooner have written* Alice in Wonderland *than the whole* Encyclopedia Britannica.*" The following selection, which contains some British and Canadian idioms and vocabulary and uses the British style of punctuation, illustrates his mixed national background.*

◆ PREVIEWING THE STORY

Look at the picture, the title, and the first paragraph of the story. Answer the questions, explaining each answer.

1. Where does the story take place?
2. Why do you think the man seems nervous?
3. What does the word *rattle* in the first paragraph mean? What other definitions do you know?
4. Do you think the man is dealing with a large amount of money? What kind of "financial career" might this story be about?

◆ THINKING ABOUT THE TOPIC

Think about and answer the following questions.

1. In your country, where is the safest place to put your savings?
2. Do you feel comfortable making transactions in banks? Why or why not?

When I go into a bank I get rattled.[1] The clerks rattle me; the wickets[2] rattle me; the sight of the money rattles me; everything rattles me.

The moment I cross the threshold[3] of a bank and attempt to transact[4] business there, I become an irresponsible[5] idiot.

I knew this beforehand, but my salary had been raised to fifty dollars a month and I felt that the bank was the only place for it.

So I shambled[6] in and looked timidly[7] round at the clerks. I had an idea that a person about to* open an account must needs* consult the manager.

I went up to a wicket marked 'Accountant.' The accountant was a tall, cool devil. The very sight of him rattled me. My voice was sepulchral.[8]

'Can I see the manager?' I said, and added solemnly, 'alone.' I don't know why I said 'alone.'

'Certainly,' said the accountant, and fetched him.[9]

The manager was a grave,[10] calm man. I held my fifty-six dollars clutched in a crumpled[11] ball in my pocket.

'Are you the manager?' I said. God knows I didn't doubt it.

'Yes,' he said.

'Can I see you,' I asked, 'alone?' I didn't want to say 'alone' again, but without it the thing seemed self-evident.[12]

The manager looked at me in some alarm.[13] He felt that I had an awful[14] secret to reveal.

'Come in here,' he said, and led the way* to a private room. He turned the key in the lock.

'We are safe from interruption here,' he said: 'sit down.'

We both sat down and looked at each other. I found no voice to speak.

'You are one of Pinkerton's men,* I presume,'[15] he said.

He had gathered[16] from my mysterious manner that I was a detective. I knew what he was thinking, and it made me worse.

'No, not from Pinkerton's,' I said, seeming to imply[17] that I came from a rival[18] agency.

[1] confused, nervous
[2] bank tellers' windows
[3] doorway, entrance
[4] conduct
[5] undependable
[6] walked unsteadily, shuffled along
[7] shyly, fearfully
[8] sad, solemn
[9] brought
[10] very serious
[11] crushed together
[12] clear, obvious
[13] fear
[14] very bad, terrible
[15] suppose, assume
[16] got an idea or impression
[17] suggest
[18] competing

'To tell the truth,' I went on, as if I had been prompted to lie about it, 'I am not a detective at all. I have come to open an account. I intend[19] to keep all my money in this bank.'

[19] plan

The manager looked relieved but still serious: he concluded now that I was a son of Baron Rothschild or a young Gould.[20]

[20] an American millionaire

'A large account, I suppose,' he said.

'Fairly large,' I whispered. 'I propose to deposit fifty-six dollars now and fifty dollars a month regularly.'

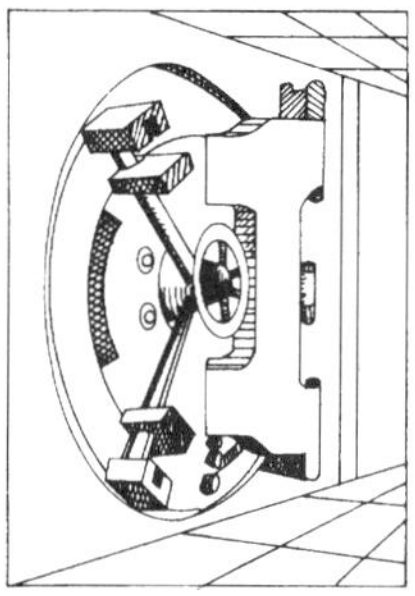

safe

The manager got up and opened the door. He called to the accountant.

'Mr. Montgomery,' he said unkindly loud, 'this gentleman is opening an account, he will deposit fifty-six dollars. Good morning.'

I rose.

A big iron door stood open at the side of the room.

'Good morning,' I said, and stepped into the safe.°

'Come out,' said the manager coldly,[21] and showed me the other way.

[21] in an unfriendly way

I went up to the accountant's wicket and poked the ball of money at him with a quick convulsive[22] movement as if I were doing a conjuring[23] trick.

[22] violently shaking

[23] magical

My face was ghastly[24] pale.

[24] ghostly; horribly

'Here,' I said, 'deposit it.' The tone of the words seemed to mean, 'Let us do this painful thing while the fit[25] is on us.'

[25] mood

He took the money and gave it to another clerk.

He made me write the sum on a slip and sign my name in a book. I no longer knew what I was doing. The bank swam before my eyes.*

'Is it deposited?' I asked in a hollow, vibrating voice.

'It is,' said the accountant.

'Then I want to draw a cheque.*

My idea was to draw out* six dollars of it for present use. Someone gave me a cheque-book through a wicket and someone else began telling me how to write it out. The people in the bank had the impression that I was an invalid millionaire. I wrote something on the cheque and thrust[26] it in at the clerk. He looked at it.

[26] pushed with force

'What! are you drawing it all out again?' he asked in surprise. Then I realized that I had written fifty-six instead of six. I was too far gone* to reason now. I had a feeling it was impossible to explain the thing. All the clerks had stopped writing to look at me.

Reckless[27] with misery, I made a plunge.*

'Yes, the whole thing.'

'You withdraw your money from the bank?'

'Every cent of it.'

'Are you not going to deposit any more?' said the clerk, astonished.[28]

'Never.'

An idiot[29] hope struck me that they might think something had insulted me while I was writing the cheque and that I had changed my mind. I made a wretched[30] attempt to look like a man with a fearfully[31] quick temper.

The clerk prepared to pay the money.

'How will you have it?' he said.

'What?'

'How will you have it?'

'Oh'—I caught his meaning* and answered without even trying to think—'in fifties.'

He gave me a fifty-dollar bill.

'And the six?' he asked dryly.

'In sixes,' I said.

He gave it me and I rushed out.

As the big door swung behind me I caught the echo of a roar of laughter that went up to the ceiling of the bank. Since then I bank no more. I keep my money in cash in my trousers pocket and my savings in silver dollars in a sock. ◆

[27] careless

[28] amazed, greatly surprised

[29] foolish

[30] unsuccessful; miserable

[31] terribly; very great

Idioms and Phrases*

about to	*ready to*
must needs	*has to (not used in American English)*
led the way	*went before and showed the way, guided*
Pinkerton's men	*guards sent by a company that specializes in protecting banks; detectives*
swam before my eyes	*seemed to be moving round and round*
draw a cheque	*write a check*
draw out	*withdraw, take out*
(too) far gone	*no longer able*
made a plunge	*did something risky or difficult*
caught his meaning	*heard, understood*

Post-Reading

Comprehension

1. Why did the narrator want to open a bank account?
2. Why did he ask to see the manager?
3. Why did the manager think he was a detective?
4. What did the manager next think that he was?
5. What was the manager's reaction when he understood what the narrator really wanted?
6. What did the narrator have to do in order to open an account?
7. Why did he withdraw all his money?
8. What kinds of bills did he ask for when he withdrew his money? Why is this humorous?
9. Where does the narrator keep his money after he withdrew it from the bank?

Responding to the Story

1. Why is the story called "My Financial Career"?
2. Is the narrator young or old? Defend your opinion.
3. Does the narrator actually state why he is afraid of banks? Can you give some reasons for his fear? What kinds of situations seem to frighten him?
4. What words does the narrator use to describe the bank and the employees and their actions? What do these words show you about his feelings about banks?
5. How do you feel about the narrator as you read the story? Do you sympathize with him? Do you feel he is foolish? What makes you feel as you do?
6. Do you—or does anyone you know—have feelings about banks like the narrator's? Describe these feelings and tell what you think causes them.
7. Have you ever had an experience in public that seemed embarrassing at the time? What happened?

VOCABULARY

Vocabulary Builder

Replace each word in parentheses with a word from the list that is closest to it in meaning. Use each word only once.

convulsive	irresponsible	presume	gathered
thrust	threshold	grave	self-evident
crumpled	fetched	awful	wretched
intend	ghastly	astonished	reckless

1. For a moment, the bank manager thought the bank had a/an ____________________ (terrible) problem that he was not aware of.
2. The steps involved in opening a savings account are so simple as to be ____________________ (clearly apparent).
3. The manager's expression was ____________________ (very serious).
4. People who spend more than they earn are said to be ____________________ (undependable) about money.
5. As soon as the narrator stepped over the ____________________ (doorway, entrance) of the bank, he became nervous.
6. The clerk ____________________ (got, brought) the manager.
7. All his money was ____________________ (crushed together) in his pocket.
8. His manner led the bank manager to ____________________ (suppose) that he was one of Pinkerton's men.
9. The manager then ____________________ (got the idea), incorrectly, that he was there to make a large deposit.

(Continued on next page)

10. With a quick, ____________________ (violent) movement, he gave the money to the bank teller.

11. His face was ____________________ (ghostly) pale when he deposited the money.

12. He said that he didn't ____________________ (plan) to deposit his money at the bank anymore.

13. He made a ____________________ (miserable) attempt to look brave.

14. His bank withdrawal ____________________ (greatly surprised) the clerk.

15. He ____________________ (pushed) the check at the clerk.

16. In a ____________________ (careless) frame of mind, he withdrew all his money.

Idiom Exercise

Exercise 1

Fill in the blanks with the correct phrases.

led the way
swam before (his) eyes
too far gone

1. The clerk ____________________ to the other room.
2. As he wrote his name, the bank ____________________ .
3. He was ____________________ to think clearly.
4. The manager ____________________ out of the safe.
5. The room ____________________ as his dizziness increased.
6. Practically from the moment he entered the bank, he was ____________________ to open an account.

Exercise 2

Write three sentences of your own, one for each idiom.

1. ____
2. ____
3. ____

Word Forms

Fill in the blanks with the correct form of the words listed.

1. responsible, irresponsible, responsibilities
   a. Opening a savings account is a very ____________________ way to deal with money.
   b. When you open a bank account, both you and the bank have certain ____________________.
   c. Some people don't save because they have ____________________ attitudes about money, while others don't save because they don't have the money.
2. doubt, doubted, doubtful
   a. It is ____________________ whether I will walk into a bank again.
   b. There is no ____________________ in my mind that I will do a good job.
   c. After a while, the bank manager ____________________ that I was a rich man.
3. imply, implied, implication
   a. I'm not trying to ____________________ anything.
   b. He resented the ____________________ that he was poor.
   c. When he asked to see the bank manager privately, he ____________________ that he was rich.
4. swam, swimmer, swimming
   a. ____________________ is healthy, invigorating, and enjoyable.
   b. You can see he is a good ____________________.
   c. Everything in the room ____________________ before my eyes.
5. intended, intentions, intending
   a. The clerk asked, "What are your ____________________ concerning opening an account?"
   b. I ____________________ to make a deposit, but I made a withdrawal instead.
   c. What are you ____________________ to do with the money you earn?
6. impressed, impression, impressive
   a. The new bank customer did not look ____________________ in any way.
   b. For a few minutes, he ____________________ the bank manager.
   c. The other bank customers were under the ____________________ that he was a millionaire.
7. interrupt, interrupting, interruption
   a. The manager became annoyed at the ____________________.
   b. I hope I'm not ____________________ anything.
   c. Please don't ____________________ me when I'm speaking.

STRUCTURE

Spelling

Exercise 1

Add -ing to the following words, using the correct spelling.

EXAMPLES: step + ing = stepping
realize + ing = realizing

a. stare + ing
b. presume + ing
c. rise + ing
d. snap + ing
e. propose + ing
f. sit + ing
g. attempt + ing
h. write + ing
i. swim + ing
j. crumple + ing
k. plunge + ing

Exercise 2

Give the plural form of the following words, using the correct spelling.

EXAMPLE: story + s = stories

a. salary + s
b. life + s
c. misery + s
d. key + s
e. agency + s
f. echo + s
g. fifty + s
h. mystery + s
i. six + s
j. business + s
k. gentleman + s

It's and *Its*

Use *it's* only when you can substitute *it is.* Do not confuse the possessive pronoun *its* (belonging to *it*) with the contraction *it's* (= *it is*).

Exercise 1

Fill in the correct form, either it's *or* its.

EXAMPLE: The manager said, "___It's___ important for a bank to take care of ___it's___ depositors."

1. A checking account is very useful because ____________ possible to withdraw money without going to the bank.
2. ____________ incredible that such deposits can be handled so quickly.

3. What impressed me most about the bank was __________________ high ceilings.
4. The problem with advice is that __________________ usually unwanted.
5 Bankers feel __________________ important for their depositors to read their monthly statements.
6. __________________ clear to see that the ATM is a great invention, although some people feel __________________ disadvantages outweigh __________________ advantages.
7. The organization held __________________ convention in a small hotel.
8. The United States encourages __________________ citizens to buy U.S. Savings Bonds.
9. __________________ a wonder that the bank didn't lose __________________ money after a guard left the safe open.

Exercise 2

Write five of your own sentences using either it's *or* its.

1. ____
2. ____
3 ____
4. ____
5. ____

Combining Sentences with *And*

Exercise 1

Combine each of the following pairs of sentences into one sentence with and. *When you combine two sentences into one compound sentence, place a comma before the* and *which connects the two sentences. In combining the sentences, eliminate as many words as possible. Remember, you do not need a comma before* and *if the sentence is not a compound sentence.*

EXAMPLES: The clerk led the way. The customer followed.
The clerk led the way, and the customer followed.

His behavior amazed the clerks. It amazed the other customers.
His behavior amazed the clerks and the other customers.

1. I crossed the threshold of a bank. I attempted to transact business.
2. My salary had been raised to fifty dollars a month. I felt that the bank was the only place for it.
3. I shambled in. I looked timidly at the clerks.

(Continued on next page)

4. We both sat down. We looked at each other.
5. I knew what he was thinking. It made me feel worse.
6. I propose to deposit fifty-six dollars now. I propose to deposit fifty dollars a month regularly.
7. The manager got up. He opened the door.
8. He made me write the sum on a slip. He made me sign my name in a book.
9. Someone gave me a checkbook through a window. Someone else began telling me how to write it out.
10. I hoped that they might think something had insulted me while I was writing the check. I hoped that they might think that I had changed my mind.
11. I keep my money in cash in my trousers pocket. I keep my savings in silver dollars in a sock.

Exercise 2

Ask a classmate to describe the process of opening a bank account. Tape-record or write down what he or she says. Summarize the process, using and *to combine some of the sentences.*

Subject-Verb Agreement

Circle the correct word in parentheses

1. The woman, as well as most of her children, (try/tries) to save money.
2. I (want/wants) to make a deposit.
3. Two tellers (was/were) late today.
4. The company (have/has) decided to go out of business.
5. Each person with a bank card (has/have) a checking account.
6. He (feel/feels) nervous in a bank.
7. Each person in here (has/have) a savings account.
8. The girls and their friend (keep/keeps) money under the mattress.
9. There (has/have) been several calls for you.
10. Neither he nor they (wish/wishes) to make trouble.

Regular and Irregular Past Tense Verbs

Change the sentences from present to past tense, making sure to use the correct verb forms.

Example: The bank clerks rattle me, and I become an irresponsible idiot.
The bank clerks rattled me, and I became an irresponsible idiot.

1. I know this, but I feel the bank is the only place for it.
2. I hold my fifty-six dollars clutched in a crumpled ball.

3. He feels that I have an awful secret to reveal.
4. He leads the way to a private room and turns the key in the lock.
5. "Good morning," I say, and step into the safe.
6. I write something on the check and thrust it in at the clerk.
7. As the big door swings behind me, I catch the echo of a roar of laughter that goes up to the ceiling of the bank.
8. I bank no more, but keep my money in my trousers pocket.

Adjectives

Exercise 1

Adjectives are used effectively to help describe the narrator's problems. Imagine yourself in a difficult, public situation like the narrator's. Write a paragraph using adjectives to help describe your problems. Use at least some of these adjectives from the story:

astonished	awful	timid
wretched	reckless	painful
grave	pale	

Exercise 2

In a group of three students, exchange paragraphs. Choose one of the three descriptive paragraphs to write as a dialogue. After your group writes the dialogue, act it out for the class.

Cloze Exercise

Fill in the blanks with the appropriate word.

Banks ____________ (1) me. When I ____________ (2) the threshold of a bank, I get an ____________ (3) feeling. Everything ____________ (4) before my eyes, ____________ (5) I turn ____________ (6) pale. I sometimes even ____________ (7) my own name. ____________ (8) therefore very difficult for me to ____________ (9) business there. For instance, when I intend ____________ (10) a deposit, I ____________ (11) the money instead. It ____________ (12) the only way to avoid the ____________ (13) of ____________ (14) to the bank is to keep my money under the mattress.

FOLLOW UP

Topics for Discussion

1. Although the narrator decides that he can do without banks, banks have a number of advantages. What do you consider some of the main advantages of banks?
2. Do you have a bank account? Is it a savings or a checking account? What are the differences between savings and checking accounts? How do you make deposits to and withdrawals from your accounts?
3. In addition to savings and checking accounts, banks offer a number of other services, including ATM cards, credit cards, mortgages, education and other loans, life insurance, safe-deposit boxes, and investment services. How many of these services are you familiar with? Can you explain what they are?
4. Today many of the functions of tellers are being taken over by ATMs (automated teller machines). It is predicted that within a few years, there may be no need for human tellers. What are the advantages and disadvantages of ATMs and of tellers? Which do you prefer? Why?
5. Part of the narrator's problem seems to be that he is too concerned about what other people in the bank might be thinking of him. Have you ever been in a situation where you were overly concerned with what people were thinking, and has this concern prevented you from doing something?

Topics for Writing

1. Have you ever been embarrassed in public? In a three-paragraph essay, describe the embarrassing event and how you handled it.
2. Fill out the sample check and bank forms on pages 53 and 54.
3. In a two-paragraph essay, compare and contrast the banks in your country with the banks in the United States. Topics can include the extent to which people use banks, the services provided, the most commonly used services, the number of banks, bank hours, the use of tellers and ATMs, the treatment of customers, and so on.
4. The story gives the narrator's thoughts. How might the incident have seemed to the accountant, to one of the clerks, or to another customer? Retell the story, more briefly but still humorously, using as your narrator one of the other people who were in the bank. Describe the mysterious customer, his actions, and your reactions.
5. Suppose that the narrator hadn't made the mistake of withdrawing all his money. What might have happened next month when he went to deposit his fifty dollars? Would the bank still rattle him? Write a short story about his second visit to the bank.

American STATE BANK

MATTHEW A. SWANN
18 Chelsea Place
New York, N.Y. 10011

NO. 159

____________ 19 ____

PAY TO THE ORDER OF ________________________ $ ______

____________________________________ DOLLARS

⑆732-0313⑆ 75 47681⑈ ________________

American STATE BANK

MATTHEW A. SWANN

__________________ 19 ____

CASH		$	
CHECKS			
	TOTAL		

⑆732-0313⑆ 75 47681⑈ **CHECKING ACCOUNT DEPOSIT TICKET**

MIDLAND BANK

SAVINGS DEPOSIT

_______________ OFFICE DATE _______________

DEPOSIT FOR THE ACCOUNT OF ▼

____

____

MY ACCOUNT NUMBER IS

			▪▪▪						▪▪▪	

PLEASE ENDORSE EACH CHECK	DOLLARS	CENTS
CASH		
COIN		
CHECKS AS FOLLOWS ON:		
TOTAL ▶		

DO NOT WRITE BELOW THIS LINE

MIDLAND BANK

SAVINGS WITHDRAWAL

NON-NEGOTIABLE

_______________ OFFICE DATE _______________

PAY THE SUM OF . . . . $_______________

_______________________________________ DOLLARS

MY ACCOUNT NUMBER IS

			▪▪▪						▪▪▪	

TO: _______________________________________

ACCOUNT OWNER SIGNATURE

____

ADDRESS

UNIT 5

Old Country Advice to the American Traveler

—WILLIAM SAROYAN

ABOUT THE AUTHOR

WILLIAM SAROYAN *(1908–1981) was born in Fresno, California, of Armenian parents. Known for his touching and sentimental stories praising personal freedom, America, and life in general, he tried almost every kind of writing: short stories, plays, and novels. He first won fame with a collection of stories,* The Daring Young Man on the Flying Trapeze *(1934), and later with the play* The Time of Your Life *(1939), for which he was awarded—and refused to accept—the Pulitzer Prize in 1940. His collection of stories,* My Name Is Aram *(1940), reflected the experiences of growing up as an Armenian-American in California's San Joaquin Valley. Saroyan served in the army during World War II and returned to California, where he lived until his death. This selection is taken from* My Name Is Aram, *and the accompanying illustration is from the original edition of the book.*

◆ PREVIEWING THE STORY

Look at the picture, the title, and the first paragraph of the story. Answer the questions, explaining each answer.

1. Where are the people in the picture and what are they doing?
2. When do you think this story takes place? How can you tell?
3. What do you think "Old Country Advice" in the title means?

◆ THINKING ABOUT THE TOPIC

Think about and answer the following questions.

1. How have you traveled between cities in your country? between cities in the United States?
2. What do you enjoy most about train travel? What do you dislike?
3. What do you think are some possible dangers of traveling by train?
4. When you travel, do you tend to talk to or avoid other passengers?

One year my uncle Melik traveled from Fresno to New York. Before he got aboard the train his uncle Garro paid him a visit* and told him about the dangers of travel.

When you get on the train, the old man said, choose your seat carefully, sit down, and do not look about.*

Yes, sir, my uncle said.

Several moments after the train begins to move, the old man said, two men wearing uniforms will come down the aisle and ask you for your ticket. Ignore them. They will be impostors.[1]

How will I know? my uncle said.

You will know, the old man said. You are no longer a child.

Yes, sir, my uncle said.

Before you have traveled twenty miles an amiable[2] young man will come to you and offer you a cigarette. Tell him you don't smoke. The cigarette will be doped.[3]

Yes, sir, said my uncle.

On your way to the diner a very beautiful young woman will bump into* you intentionally[4] and almost embrace you, the old man said. She will be extremely apologetic[5] and attractive[6] and your natural impulse[7] will be to cultivate[8] her friendship. Dismiss your natural impulse and go on in and eat. The woman will be an adventuress.[9]

A what? my uncle said.

A whore,[10] the old man shouted. Go on in and eat. Order the best food, and if the diner is crowded, and the beautiful young woman sits across the table from you, do not look into her eyes. If she speaks, pretend to be deaf.[11]

Yes, sir, my uncle said.

Pretend to be deaf, the old man said. That is the only way out of it.*

Out of what? my uncle said.

Out of the whole ungodly[12] mess, the old man said. I have traveled. I know what I'm talking about.

Yes, sir, my uncle said.

Let's say no more about it, the old man said.

Yes, sir, my uncle said.

Let's not speak of the matter again, the old man said. It's finished. I have seven children. My life has been a full and righteous[13] one. Let's not

[1] people pretending to be what they are not

[2] friendly

[3] full of a drug or narcotic

[4] on purpose

[5] full of regrets

[6] pretty

[7] feeling

[8] develop

[9] a woman who seeks to earn money dishonestly

[10] prostitute

[11] unable to hear

[12] shameful

[13] just, godly

give it another thought. I have land, vines, trees, cattle, and money. One cannot have everything—except for a day or two at a time.

Yes, sir, my uncle said.

On your way back to your seat from the diner, the old man said, you will pass through the smoker.[14] There you will find a game of cards in progress.* The players will be three middle-aged men with expensive-looking rings on their fingers. They will nod at you pleasantly and one of them will invite you to join the game. Tell them, No speak English.

[14] railway car in which passengers may smoke

Yes, sir, my uncle said.

That is all, the old man said.

Thank you very much, my uncle said.

One thing more, the old man said. When you go to bed at night, take your money out of your pocket and put it in your shoe. Put your shoe under your pillow, keep your head on the pillow all night, *and don't sleep.*

Yes, sir, my uncle said.

That is all, the old man said.

The old man went away and the next day my uncle Melik got aboard the train and traveled straight across America to New York. The two men in uniforms were not impostors, the young man with the doped cigarette did not arrive, the beautiful young woman did not sit across the table from my uncle in the diner, and there was no card game in progress in the smoker. My uncle put his money in his shoe and put his shoe under his pillow and put his head on the pillow and didn't sleep all night the first night, but the second night he abandoned[15] the whole ritual.[16]

[15] gave up, stopped

[16] routine ceremony

The second day he *himself* offered another young man a cigarette which the other young man accepted. In the diner my uncle went out of his way to sit at a table with a young lady. He started a poker game in the smoker, and long before the train ever got to New York my uncle knew everybody aboard[17] the train and everybody knew him. Once, while the train was traveling through Ohio, my uncle and the young man who had accepted the cigarette and two young ladies on their way to Vassar[18] formed a quartet and sang *The Wabash Blues.*

[17] on, in

[18] a college in New York State

The journey was a very pleasant one.

When my uncle Melik came back from New York, his old uncle Garro visited him again.

I see you are looking all right, he said. Did you follow my instructions?

Yes, sir, my uncle said.

The old man looked far away in space.

I am please that *someone* has profited by my experience, he said. ◆

IDIOMS AND PHRASES*

paid him a visit	*came to see him*
look about	*look all around*
bump into	*walk into; accidentally meet*
way out of it	*solution (to the problem)*
in progress	*happening, going on*

POST-READING

Understanding the Story

1. What advice did Uncle Garro give Melik?
2. Why did Uncle Garro warn him?
3. What strangers did Uncle Garro tell Melik to stay away from?
4. Where did Uncle Garro tell Melik to hide his money?
5. Did Melik follow Uncle Garro's advice? How do you know?
6. Why was Melik's journey a pleasant one?

Responding to the Story

1. Did Uncle Garro really expect Melik to take his advice? How do you know?
2. Would Melik have enjoyed his trip as much if he had followed Uncle Garro's advice? Why or why not? How would his trip have been different?
3. What made Uncle Garro think of the specific dangers he described to Melik?
4. Can you explain the ending? Why did Melik lie to Uncle Garro? Did Uncle Garro believe him?
5. Do you think Uncle Garro followed his own advice when he was young? Give reasons for your answer.
6. Did you ever have an experience similar to Melik's, in which a parent or other older relative gave you advice before you went off on a trip? What advice did they give you? To what extent did you follow their advice?

VOCABULARY

Vocabulary Builder

Circle the letter of the word or phrase that defines the underlined word in each sentence.

1. Uncle Garro was concerned that his nephew might get into an ungodly mess.
   a. shameful c. tragic
   b. doubtful d. gloomy

2. After one day Melik abandoned the ritual.
   a. silence c. advice
   b. mess d. routine

3. He abandoned the plan because it wasn't practical.
   a. disliked c. gave up
   b. fought against d. changed

4. On Melik's train, the people collecting the tickets were not impostors.
   a. pretenders c. workers in uniform
   b. professionals d. students

5. Uncle Garro's life had been a righteous one.
   a. difficult c. old-fashioned
   b. full d. just

6. Melik never met the attractive, apologetic, and deceitful young lady that Uncle Garro warned him against.
   a. full of sympathy c. full of regrets
   b. careless d. lying

7. In the diner Melik intentionally sat next to a young lady.
   a. happily c. without knowing
   b. quickly d. on purpose

8. Uncle Garro thought that Melik's impulses would get him into trouble.
   a. feelings c. areas of ignorance
   b. words d. desires to please others

Idiom Exercise

Exercise 1

Circle the letter of the correct definition for each underlined idiom.

1. Uncle Garro decided to pay him a visit.
   a. offer him advice c. go to see him
   b. give him money for the trip d. see him again

2. A card game was in progress in the smoker.
   a. moving forward rapidly c. beginning
   b. happening d. ending

3. Uncle Garro saw only one way out of it.
   a. problem c. solution
   b. danger d. lesson

Exercise 2

Write a sentence of your own for each of the idioms.

1. ____________________
2. ____________________
3. ____________________

STRUCTURE

Adjectives and Adverbs

Fill in the blanks with the correct words in parentheses.

EXAMPLE: The journey was a very ___*pleasant*___ one.
(pleasant/pleasantly)

1. Uncle Garro undoubtedly considered himself a ____________ traveler.
   (well/good)
2. Melik didn't sleep ____________ his first night on the train.
   (well/good)
3. Melik chose his seat ____________.
   (careful/carefully)
4. He was also ____________ about where he put his money.
   (careful/carefully)

(Continued on next page)

5. Someone who wants to meet a particular person might bump into that person ____________________.
(intentional/intentionally)
6. Uncle Garro advised Melik, "Dismiss your ____________________
(natural/naturally)
impulse and go on in and eat."
7. Melik's abandoning his uncle's advice was quite ____________________.
(intentional/intentionally)
8. According to Uncle Garro, a woman who looked ____________________
(attractive/attractively)
might nonetheless turn out to be an adventuress.
9. The people Melik met on the train seemed ____________________ and
(amiable/amiably)
actually were as they seemed.
10. The young men nodded at Melik ____________________.
(pleasant/pleasantly)
11. The young people were ____________________ friendly.
(particular/particularly)
12. The quartet sang ____________________.
(beautiful/beautifully)

Imperatives

When Uncle Garro gives advice, he often does so in imperative sentences. An imperative sentence is one that issues a command or gives instructions. For example, *Choose your seat carefully, sit down, and do not look about* is a sentence from the story that actually contains three imperatives.

Exercise 1

Read the story again and find the imperative sentences. Write eight of these sentences below.

1. ____________________
2. ____________________
3. ____________________
4. ____________________
5. ____________________
6. ____________________
7. ____________________
8. ____________________

Exercise 2

Pretend that you are giving advice to someone who is traveling to a place you know. Give this person some advice in a paragraph that includes imperatives.

Sentences with *Let's*

Uncle Garro also uses a form that is closely related to imperatives: sentences with *let's (let us)*. Sentences with *let's* are used to make commands, requests, or suggestions in which the speaker includes himself or herself. For example, Uncle Garro says, *Let's say no more about it.*

Exercise 1

Rewrite the imperatives as suggestions including the speaker; use let's.

1. Don't speak of the matter again.
2. Don't give it another thought.
3. Sit down and do not look around.
4. Go in and eat.
5. If she speaks, pretend to be deaf.

Exercise 2

Pretend that a friend is visiting you for the day, and you are planning the day's activities. Give your plan for the day in a paragraph, using some sentences with let's.

Combining Sentences by Using Relative Pronouns

Combine the following sentences by using which *or* who.

Use who *or* whom *to refer to people.*

EXAMPLE: The two young ladies attracted our attention. They were on their way to Vassar.
The two young ladies *who* attracted our attention were on their way to Vassar.

Use which *to refer to things or animals.*

EXAMPLE: An amiable young man will offer you a cigarette. It will be doped.
An amiable young man will offer you a cigarette *which* will be doped.

1. The tall man looks like an impostor. He is wearing a blue shirt.
2. Melik saw the young lady. She was sitting in the diner.
3. Melik offered another young man a cigarette. He accepted it.
4. The trip was finally approved. We discussed it yesterday.
5. The man ran to the train. He was in a hurry.
6. Some strangers are dangerous. They look very safe.
7. The travelers were running down the street. They were holding hands.
8. Melik and his friend walked to the station. They were carrying suitcases.
9. Tip the porter generously. He carries your luggage.
10. The seat belongs to the young lady. The seat is near the window.

Quotation Marks

Exercise 1

As you may have noted, the story does not contain any quotation marks. Use quotation marks to enclose only a **direct quotation**: one that repeats a person's exact words.

The following three general principles apply to most quotations:

1. Capitalize the first word of every direct quotation, wherever it may come, because it is the first word of the speaker's sentence.
2. Put a comma between the quotation and any explanatory words like *he said*.
3. Always put the comma or the period *before* the closing quotation marks (," or .").

In the following passage, put quotation marks to indicate direct speech.

EXAMPLES: Let's say no more about it, the old man said.
Yes, sir, my uncle said.
"Let's say no more about it," the old man said.
"Yes, sir," my uncle said.

Let's not speak of the matter again, the old man said. It's finished. I have seven children. My life has been a full and righteous one. Let's not give it another thought. I have land, vines, trees, cattle, and money. One cannot have everything—except for a day or two at a time.

Yes, sir, my uncle said.

On your way back to your seat from the diner, the old man said, you will pass through the smoker. There you will find a game of cards in progress. The players will be three middle-aged men with expensive-looking rings on their fingers. They will nod at you pleasantly and one of them will invite you to join the game. Tell them, No speak English.

Yes, sir, my uncle said.

That is all, the old man said.

Thank you very much, my uncle said.

One thing more, the old man said. When you go to bed at night, take your money out of your pocket and put it in your shoe. Put your shoe under your pillow, keep your head on the pillow all night, *and don't sleep.*

Exercise 2

With a classmate, write a short story in which you plan a two-week vacation with the help of a travel agent. The story can be humorous, but it doesn't have to be. Include a conversation between you and the travel agent—for example, on the means of transportation you will use (train, airplane, bus), hotel reservations, car rentals, and prices. Be sure to use quotation marks, other punctuation marks, and capitalization correctly, in keeping with the rules for quotation.

When you are finished, you can read the story to the class, acting out the conversation.

Prepositions of Time and Place

Answer the questions in complete sentences, using at least one of the following prepositions in each sentence:

on	under
through	over
between	near
inside	from
at	for
to	by
in	after
before	with

You may use a preposition more than once, and you do not need to use all the prepositions.

1. When did Uncle Garro visit Melik the first time?
2. Where did Melik travel?
3. Where was Melik supposed to put his money?
4. Where was Melik supposed to put his shoe?
5. How did Melik travel from Fresno to New York?
6. When did Melik follow Uncle Garro's instructions, and when did he abandon them?
7. Where did Melik eat?
8. Where did Melik sit while eating?
9. When did Uncle Garro visit Melik the second time?
10. Where did you last travel on vacation? When did you travel? For how long?
11. Where else have you traveled? Where have you lived? When did you live there?
12. Give directions on how to get to the train station from your home and explain where the train station is located. (If necessary, use prepositions in addition to those listed.)

FOLLOW UP

Topics for Discussion

1. Compare airplane travel with train travel. Which do you prefer? Why?
2. What do you think are the dangers of travel today? If Uncle Garro were speaking to Melik today, what advice might he give him?
3. What suggestions do you have for improving train travel today?
4. What are the advantages and disadvantages of traveling alone?
5. How helpful is the advice that older people have to offer younger people? How likely are younger people to follow such advice? Explain your opinions.
6. ***ROLE PLAY:*** Pretend you are Uncle Garro. What advice would you give Melik regarding train travel? Have a classmate take the role of Melik.

Topics for Writing

1. Write a short story about a long journey that you have taken. What were your most memorable adventures on that journey?
2. Imagine that you can visit anywhere in the world. Describe where you would go and what your trip there would be like.
3. In a three-paragraph essay, describe the most memorable character you have ever met on your travels.
4. When you are choosing a seat on a train or a plane, what kind of person would you not want to sit next to? Why? List your reasons in a two-paragraph essay.
5. Pretend you are Melik. Write several diary entries describing your train trip to New York. In writing these entries, build on the brief information that is given in the story.

UNIT 6

This Year It's Going to Be Different

—WILL STANTON

About the Author

Will Stanton *(1918–) is a humorist and a magazine writer. He has published more than 150 articles in such magazines as* Reader's Digest, McCall's, *and* The New Yorker. *Some of his stories have been made into films; one of them is Walt Disney's* Charlie and the Angel, *which is based on a story from the collection* The Golden Evenings of Summer *(1971). The following story, retitled "Happy New Year, Mrs. Robinson," appears in his collection* The Old Familiar Booby Traps of Home *(1978).*

◆ Previewing the Story

Look at the picture, the title, and the first paragraph of the story. Answer the questions, explaining each answer.

1. What is the relationship of the man in the center of the picture to the other people shown?
2. What kind of mood does the man seem to be in? What moods do the other people seem to be in?
3. How would you connect the picture to the title and first paragraph? Do you think the scene it shows takes place before or after the New Year begins?

◆ Thinking about the Topic

Think about and answer the following questions.

1. How is the New Year celebrated in your country? Are New Year's resolutions made?
2. Do you make New Year's resolutions? Are your resolutions successful?

New Year's resolutions* are like anything else—you get out of them what you put in. Judging from results other years, I had never put enough in, but this year was going to be different. I read books on self-improvement before I wrote my list. Find some beauty in everything.... Make the other fellow feel important.... About thirty like that. Pretty clearly, anyone who followed my collection of rules would be blessed with a richer life, boundless[1] love from his family, and the admiration of the community. I could hardly wait until New Year's Day.

[1] unlimited

When I came downstairs Maggie, my wife, was at the kitchen sink. I tiptoed over and kissed her on the back of the neck. (Resolution No. 1: Be spontaneous[2] in showing affection.) She shrieked[3] and dropped a cup. "Don't ever sneak up* on me like that again!" she cried.

[2] unplanned, natural
[3] made a loud cry

"You're looking lovely this morning," I said. (A sincere compliment is worth its weight in gold.)*

"Look," she said, "it wasn't my idea to stay out until four a.m."

I took some aspirin and coffee into the living room. I'd just started reading the paper when Sammy, our five-year-old, came in. He was wearing the watch he'd received for Christmas. "Say, Dad," he said, "what makes a watch run?"[4]

[4] operate; work

In the old days* I would have told him to ask his mother. Instead, I got a pencil and drew a sketch[5] of the escapement mechanism.° (Always encourage your child's curiosity.) It took about fifteen minutes, and Sammy wandered off several times, but I kept calling him back. "There," I said, "that's what makes your watch run."

[5] drawing, diagram

escapement mechanism

"Then how come* it doesn't?" he asked.

His brother Roy walked by. "You have to wind[6] it," said Roy. Sammy wound it and held it to his ear. He smiled. "Roy sure is smart," he said.

[6] tighten the working parts by turning

Our daughter Gretchen came in with her doll, Mrs. Robinson. "Good morning, Gretchen," I said. "Happy New Year, Mrs. Robinson." (Meet your child at his own level.)

"It isn't either happy," said Gretchen. "Mrs. Robinson is sick. Probably a coronary."[7]

[7] heart attack

"Why don't you take her to see Dr. Sammy?" I suggested. "He can use his new doctor's kit."[8]

[8] set of instruments

The phone rang, and I answered it. It was a friend of our daughter Kit. "Happy New Year, Marilyn," I said. "What have you been doing over the holidays?" (Show an interest in your children's friends.) She said she hadn't been doing anything much. "Come now, a pretty girl like you," I said jovially[9]—"I'll bet the fellows are swarming[10] around. . . . What's that? Yes, of course you can speak to Kit. Certainly."

[9] merrily
[10] crowding

Kit was in her room with the record player going very loud. I rapped[11] on the door. She called out something, and I went in. She was in her pajamas. "I didn't say you could come in!" she yelled, grabbing[12] a robe and holding it in front of her. At fourteen, she has become extremely[13] aware of being female.

[11] knocked loudly
[12] taking suddenly
[13] greatly, very

"I'm sorry. I couldn't understand you," I said apologetically. To ease the situation,* I picked up her brand-new[14] sweater from the floor and put it over a chair.

[14] newly purchased

"I was going to pick it up," she said defensively.[15] "You don't always put *your* things away."

[15] protectively

There was a series[16] of shrieks down the hall. I found Gretchen in tears. Roy and Sammy were about to* perform open-heart surgery on Mrs. Robinson with a scout knife.° "She told us Mrs. Robinson was sick," Roy said.

[16] several, one following the other

scout knife

I suggested that they carve[17] something for their mother—like a salad spoon. (Encourage creativity[18] in the young.)

[17] cut into a shape with a knife
[18] artistic expression

In the kitchen, Maggie wanted to know what was wrong with Gretchen. "Mrs. Robinson had a coronary," I told her.

"I know you're not feeling your best after last night," she said, "but I'm getting a little tired of these smart[19] remarks. Would you mind taking the garbage out?"

[19] rude, disrespectful

"I'd be happy to," I said. (The most trivial[20] chore[21] can prove rewarding if approached with zest.)[22]

"Do you have to be so sarcastic?"[23] she said.

[20] unimportant
[21] small job
[22] sharp enjoyment
[23] bitter, nasty

It seemed that my resolutions weren't working the way the books had said. I didn't quit, though. I helped the boys build a snowman—only Sammy got his feet wet and Roy lost his mittens and they went inside. I played jacks[24] with Gretchen, but she said I didn't do it right. I struck up* a conversation with Kit, trying to establish some kind of rapport.[25] I touched

[24] a children's game
[25] agreement, harmony

on* hippies, pop music, dating, morality, and so on. She contributed very little. Anybody else would have thrown in the sponge,* but I kept trying. For example, Maggie always dreads[26] taking down the Christmas tree, so I thought I'd do it for her. (Take over one of your wife's chores; she'll love you for it.)

I was about two thirds done[27] when Maggie came in. "Oh no!" she cried. "I wanted it left up for the party tonight. Can't you just sit and watch a football game? Please? It's what you usually do on New Year's."

"This year is different," I said.

"Yes, isn't it?" She shook her head. "I swear I don't know. The kids have been impossible all day. I found the boys whittling[28] on my best salad spoon, and then they had the nerve[29] to say you suggested it. And Kit has been in a poisonous[30] mood. She said that Marilyn phoned and you didn't tell her. And that you cross-examined[31] Marilyn about her boyfriends."

"Hold it!" I said. "I was only making small talk."* By now the kids were in the room, drawn[32] by the commotion.[33]

"You never bothered with small talk before. Why start now?"

"Because it's New Year's," I said. I explained to the assembled gathering about the books and the resolutions and what I'd been trying to accomplish. Silence. The kids stood there looking uneasily[34] at each other. "A man wants to improve himself," I said. "He wants to be a better husband, a better father—"

"We all want to be better," Maggie said. "Except that when you're so considerate[35] it doesn't seem natural. If the kids do something and you get mad, they know where they stand.* But when you're so even-tempered—"[36]

"Yeah," Kit said. "You didn't say a word about my clothes on the floor. You just smiled. It made me sick."

Roy said, "I been[37] in more trouble today. . . . "

Gretchen said, "I think it was better when you didn't play jacks."

"And yelled," Sammy said, "and said 'damitall.'"[38]

"All right," I snarled.[39] "I make every effort* to be a good father, and this is the thanks I get. The fact is, you don't deserve the father you've got."

[26] fears greatly

[27] finished (past participle of *do*)

[28] shaping wood with a knife

[29] impoliteness; boldness

[30] very bad, angry

[31] questioned closely

[32] attracted

[33] great noise

[34] uncomfortably

[35] thoughtful of others

[36] calm

[37] *incorrect English*

[38] damn it all—mild curse

[39] growled angrily

I was illustrating my points with gestures. "You're the ones who'd better start making resolutions. Like doing your homework, cleaning your rooms, letting the spoons alone. And when I tell you to do something, jump!"

I reached out to steady[40] a lamp I had brushed with my sleeve. "Furthermore—"[41] At this moment, I realized suddenly that the atmosphere had changed. The kids were sprawled[42] on the floor, relaxed. I turned to Maggie.

"Why is everybody smiling? What's the big joke?"

"No joke," she said. "We're just happy to have you back again." ◆

[40] make stable; keep from falling
[41] also
[42] lying spread out

IDIOMS AND PHRASES*

New Year's resolutions	*promises made at New Year's to improve or reform*
sneak up	*come slowly and unnoticed*
worth its weight in gold	*very valuable*
old days	*long ago*
how come	*why*
ease the situation	*make things less tense*
about to	*ready to*
struck up	*began, started*
touched on	*spoke of briefly, mentioned*
thrown in the sponge	*admitted defeat*
making small talk	*talking about unimportant matters*
know where they stand	*know how things are; know what to expect*
make every effort	*do one's best*

POST-READING

Comprehension

1. Why was the narrator trying to improve himself?
2. What kinds of things was he going to do differently this year?
3. Name four things the narrator did to be friendly and helpful to his family.
4. How did Maggie, his wife, react to his show of affection?
5. How did Sammy get his watch to run?

6. How did Gretchen's brothers plan to heal her doll?
7. How did the narrator show an interest in Kit's friend?
8. How was Mrs. Robinson saved from open-heart surgery?
9. Why was Maggie upset when her husband took down the Christmas decorations?
10. Why is everyone smiling at the end of the story?

Responding to the Story

1. Why did the narrator read books on self-improvement before he wrote his list? Do you think his resolutions would have been more successful if he hadn't read these books?
2. Why was the narrator's family unhappy with his behavior? If you were a child in the family, which would you have preferred—his behavior after making the resolutions or his usual behavior? Explain.
3. Why doesn't the narrator's yelling frighten his family?
4. Does this family seem to be a happy family? Why or why not?
5. Do you think this story shows something about New Year's resolutions? Are New Year's resolutions doomed to failure?

VOCABULARY

Vocabulary Builder

Exercise 1

Synonyms: *Find the word in the second column that most closely matches the meaning of the word or words in the first column.*

1. small job in the home	a. sprawl
2. understanding	b. rapport
3. heart attack	c. rap
4. knock loudly	d. coronary
5. yell loudly	e. shriek
6. determination or promise to improve	f. carve
7. crowd	g. sketch
8. cut into a shape	h. swarm
9. spread out	i. chore
10. drawing	j. resolution

Exercise 2

Maggie and her daughter Kit have different personalities. Whatever Maggie does, says, or is, Kit is completely the opposite. From the following descriptions of Maggie, supply the opposite qualities (antonyms) for Kit. Choose from this list:

boundless	trivial	drawn by
spontaneous	sarcastic	considerate
smart	dreads	makes every effort
jovially		

1. Maggie has limited energy. Kit's energy is ___________________.
2. Maggie is very sweet. Kit is often ___________________.
3. Maggie always plans ahead. Kit is ___________________.
4. Maggie lets only important things bother her, but Kit often makes a fuss over ___________________ matters.
5. Maggie looks forward to meeting new people, but Kit always ___________________ these meetings.
6. Maggie sometimes gives ___________________ answers, but Kit is always respectful.
7. Maggie generally fears any kind of danger, but Kit is always ___________________ the excitement.
8. Kit is sometimes tactless and rude, but Maggie is always ___________________.
9. Kit will usually answer the telephone sadly, but Maggie will always answer it ___________________.
10. Maggie always ___________________ to keep her New Year's resolutions; Kit never makes them.

Idiom Exercise

Write your own sentences using each of the idiomatic expressions listed below.

EXAMPLE: Please don't *sneak up on* me, because it frightens me.

1. brand new

   ____

2. throw in the sponge

   ____

3. cross-examine

   ____

4. worth its weight in gold

   ____

5. strike up a conversation

   ____

6. in the old days

    ____

7. touch on

    ____

8. ease the situation

    ____

9. make small talk

    ____

10. wander off

    ____

Word Forms

Fill in the blanks with the correct form of the words listed.

1. dread, dreading, dreadful
    a. Maggie was ________________ taking down the Christmas tree.
    b. The new doll looked ________________.
    c. I always ________________ making New Year's resolutions.
2. spontaneous, spontaneously, spontaneity
    a. Children show a great deal of ________________ when they play.
    b. There was ________________ applause when Dad became his old self again.
    c. People respond ________________ to a smile.
3. performed, performing, performance
    a. Ray and Sammy ________________ complicated surgery on Mrs. Robinson.
    b. My ________________ was very amusing, I thought.
    c. The children were ________________ for a very young audience.
4. consider, considerate, considering, consideration
    a. He was ________________ whether to keep his New Year's resolutions.
    b. He was trying to be a ________________ husband.
    c. Do you ________________ him a kind father?
    d. He showed no ________________ for his daughter's feelings.

STRUCTURE

Present Perfect and Past Perfect Tenses

Exercise 1

The **present perfect tense** is used for an action that began in the past and continues in the present. It is formed with *have / has* plus the past participle of the verb.

See Unit 3 for an explanation of the past perfect tense.

Fill in the blanks with either the past perfect or present perfect form of the verbs indicated.

EXAMPLES: So far this year, I ___*have kept*___ (keep) my New Year's resolutions.

I ___*had made*___ (make) several New Year's resolutions but was not able to keep them.

1. Before this year he __________ never __________ (put) enough into New Year's resolutions and therefore __________ never __________ (get) much out of them.
2. Before he wrote his list of resolutions, he __________ (read) many books on self-improvement.
3. All day long he __________ (try) to keep his resolutions, and he is doing a good job of it.
4. For example, this morning he __________ just __________ (start) reading his newspaper when Sammy came in.
5. Sammy was wearing the watch he __________ (receive) for Christmas.
6. In the old days, he __________n't __________ (pay) much attention to Sammy's requests for information, but this time he did.

7. Nevertheless, the changes in his behavior ____________n't ____________ (please) his family, who prefer that he be his usual self.
8. "Kit ____________ (be) in a poisonous mood all day," Maggie said. "And the kids ____________ (be) impossible."
9. Sammy ____________ (be) in more trouble today than he ____________ ever ____________ (be) before.

Exercise 2

Role Play: Pretend you are giving a New Year's Eve party. Using the present perfect tense wherever possible, tell your classmates what you have done to prepare for the party.

It's and *Its*

Although very different structures, it's *and* its *are sometimes confused. Fill in the blanks with* it's *or* its. *Use* it's *only when you can substitute* it is. *Do not confuse the possessive pronoun* its *(belonging to* it*) with the contraction* it's (= it is).

EXAMPLE: He has a plan for the New Year but doesn't know if

______*it's*______ a good plan.

1. This year ____________ going to be different.
2. A sincere compliment is worth ____________ weight in gold.
3. I'm starting to make small talk now because ____________ New Year's.
4. Watch a football game—____________ what you usually do.
5. His behavior was thoughtful, but ____________ effect was to put Kit in a poisonous mood.
6. By putting the sweater in ____________ place, he offended his daughter.
7. A resolution is easy to make, but ____________ hard to stick to, especially when some of ____________ consequences are unexpected.
8. The family was happier when ____________ members were all behaving the way they had in the old days.
9. ____________ clear that the New Year's experiment was a complete failure.
10. ____________ natural to want to improve oneself, but ____________ not always wise to try.

Appositives

Appositives are phrases that follow a name or other noun and further identify or explain it. For example, in *Will Stanton, the author of this story, is well known as a humorist and magazine writer,* the phrase *the author of this story* is an appositive: It further identifies Will Stanton. Notice that appositives are set off by commas. Commas are used because appositives provide additional information and are not necessary for understanding who the noun refers to.

Exercise 1

Change the following sentences with relative clauses to sentences with appositives.

EXAMPLE: This story, which was first called "This Year It's Going to Be Different," was later renamed "Happy New Year, Mrs. Robinson."

This story, "This Year It's Going to Be Different," was later renamed "Happy New Year, Mrs. Robinson."

1. Maggie, who is my wife, was at the kitchen sink.
2. I'd just started reading the paper when Sammy, who is our five-year-old, came in.
3. His watch, which was a Christmas present, wasn't wound.
4. Roy, who is his older brother, told him that he needed to wind it.

Exercise 2

Write a paragraph about the members of your family. Give such facts as their names, ages, relationship to you, and what they do. Be sure to use some appositives where appropriate.

Sentence Combining

Combine the sentences below by following the suggested patterns.

1. I read books on self-improvement. I wrote my list.

   Before ____________________, I read ____________________.
2. Maggie is my wife. She was at the sink. I came downstairs.

   Maggie, my ____________________, ____________________ when ____________________.
3. I'd started reading the paper. Sammy came in. Sammy is our five-year-old son.

   I'd started ____________________ when Sammy, our ____________________, ____________________.

4. He was wearing a watch. He had received a watch for Christmas.

   He ____________________ that ____________________.

5. I struck up a conversation with Kit. I was trying to establish some kind of rapport.

   In order to ____________________, I struck up ____________________.

Make up your own five sentences, using each of the above patterns.

1. ____
2. ____
3. ____
4. ____
5. ____

FOLLOW UP

Topics for Discussion

1. Why do people make New Year's resolutions? In your experience, how successful are people in keeping them?
2. What kinds of New Year's resolutions have you made in the past? What kinds would you make today?
3. What kinds of New Year's resolutions would you like your parents to make? Your teachers? Your friends?
4. Have your efforts to act nicer ever been misunderstood or misinterpreted? How?
5. Why is it so hard to change our behavior, especially our behavior toward other people? Have you known people who greatly changed the way they were? What kind of changes did they make? How were they able to make these changes?

Topics for Writing

1. Write a paragraph telling what New Year's resolutions you would make and how you would go about keeping your New Year's resolutions.
2. Father tried to explain to Sammy what makes a watch run. What Sammy really wanted to know was how to work it. Write instructions explaining how to make something work; for example, how to set an alarm clock, how to operate a VCR, how to use a camera, etc.

(Continued on next page)

3. With a classmate, write a speech in which you try to get people to change their habits. For example, try to convince people to eat nutritious, well-balanced meals or to exercise. List as many reasons for self-improvement as you can.
4. Following the model in the story, list the steps you would take to improve yourself, e.g., "Show an interest in your children's friends."
5. How would your family and friends react if you suddenly changed your behavior completely because of New Year's resolutions that you had made? Write a short, humorous story, in which you start by telling your resolutions and go on to describe people's reactions.

Unit 7

A Bird in Hand—What's It Worth?

—Elaine Hart Messmer

About the Author

Elaine Hart Messmer *has contributed to many magazines and collections of short stories. This selection is taken from* The Bedside Phoenix Nest *(1965), edited by Martin Levin.*

◆ Previewing the Story

Look at the picture, the title, and the first paragraph of the story. Answer the questions, explaining each answer.

1. Does the title sound in any way familiar? What do you think it means?
2. What do you think these differently dressed people represent? Why do you think they are holding some animals while other animals are off in the distance?

◆ Thinking about the Topic

Think about and answer the following questions.

1. Would you expect different languages to have similar proverbs? Why or why not?
2. What is your favorite proverb in your language? What does it mean? Do you know if it exists in English and other languages?

When your own backyard[1] is smack[2] up against the city of Washington, D.C., as ours is, it's pretty hard to keep from wondering what's happening on the other side of the fence,[3] and especially behind the impressive doors of the magnificent mansions[4] along Embassy Row. Yet, in two decades of living almost next door to all these foreign dignitaries,[5] I'd never met any of them to speak of, or to, with the exception of one time when my car locked bumpers° with that of a Far Eastern gentleman in a race for the same parking place.

It wasn't until one day over lunch in a Chinese restaurant that I got the courage to do anything about this omission.[6] My fortune cookie° produced a slip of paper upon which was written, "Take what you've got and never want more."

I called the Chinese Embassy and asked the young lady who answered exactly what that meant. Did they really have such a proverb?[7] She replied, between giggles,[8] that the fortune cookie didn't lie; it was indeed an old Chinese proverb, and similar in meaning to our "A bird in the hand is worth two in the bush."* I told her I was so glad that we had something in common* and thanked her. She told me to "call any time."

It was then that I decided to find out if the rest of the world had this proverb in common with us. It would be a start, anyway, in neighborly[9] relations.

I had no trouble in my quest[10] at the Spanish Embassy. When I asked for the Spanish version of "A bird, etc.," the bright but highly amused young woman came up immediately with, "*Más vale pájaro en mano que cien volando*." Any Spaniard knows that that means "Better to have one in hand than a hundred flying."

On to Nepal. With all they've got to worry about these days, maybe they'd welcome a little cheerful diversion.[11] I was glad I called. Not at first, but later on. I explained my mission to the first woman who answered. She asked "*Who* is this?" and then, "*Whom* are you with?" Finally, I managed to convince her that I wasn't some gung-ho[12]

[1] piece of land behind a house

[2] directly, exactly

[3] barrier of wood or wire

[4] grand houses

[5] important people

[6] lack, something left out

[7] saying

[8] brief, silly laughter

[9] friendly, like neighbors

[10] search

[11] change, distraction

[12] (slang) foolishly enthusiastic

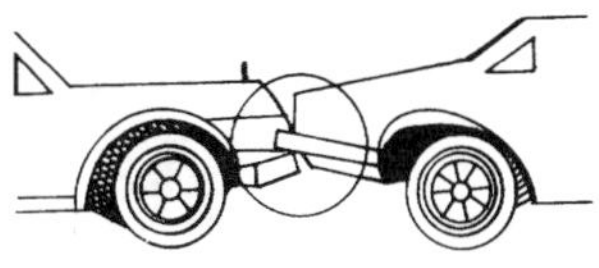
bumpers

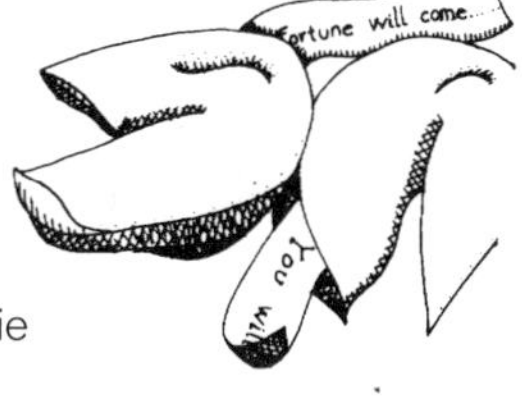
fortune cookie

ornithologist[13] who was flying high* and she turned me over to another woman. In tones ringing on the highest decibels[14] of annoyance,[15] she demanded another full explanation and then deposited the entire problem in the lap of a pleasant, cordial gentleman who *did* sound as though this might be the brightest spot in his day. He told me that Nepal assuredly[16] did have such a proverb, and did I want it in Nepalese? I told him that English would do, and he informed me that in Nepal the prudent[17] folk say, "A blind maternal[18] uncle is better than none at all."

[13] one who studies birds
[14] units of sound
[15] slight anger
[16] certainly
[17] wise
[18] related through one's mother

Well, I knew all this international goodwill was too good to last, because I really came up against it* at the French Embassy. The woman to whom I addressed my question about "A bird, etc." was extremely excitable and gave me a verbal blast* in rapid-fire[19] French. We parted on questionable terms.

[19] fast

After the French debacle,[20] I turned north to Scandinavia, where tempers are cooler. They are all pretty much in accord* and claim that "A bird in the hand is worth two in the woods . . . or on the roof . . . or in the tree." Take your pick.*

[20] catastrophe

The folk[21] in Iraq and the Somali Republic, although not exactly Scandinavians, have the same proverb.

[21] people

A very courteous[22] lady at the German Embassy told me that in Germany they feel that "The sparrow[23] in the hand is better than the pigeon[24] on the roof."

[22] polite
[23] a type of small bird
[24] a large, grayish bird seen mostly in cities

The Japanese say that it would be better not to pursue[25] two rabbits when you already have one in your hand, or you may lose all.

[25] go after

At the Embassy of Ireland, a charming gentleman with one of those O-apostrophe names felt that "sure the great wealth of Irish culture could produce a similar proverb." He took my number and called back the following morning to tell me that in Ireland "A trout[26] in the hand is better than a salmon[27] in the pool."

[26] a type of small fish
[27] a type of larger fish

Next I called Greece. I was jostled[28] upward though the chain of command* to a gentleman of cultural substance.* In Greece, he told me, they say, "It's better to have one thing in your hand than to wait for two."

[28] pushed

I really felt sorry for the poor man with whom I talked at the Italian Embassy. He had to compete with a pneumatic drill° in the background, as he tried with members of his staff to get to the bottom of* the Italian version of the proverb. First, there were two voices in excited Italian discussion, then three voices, then four. Just about the time I was ready

pneumatic drill

to give up,* he returned to the phone and shouted in triumph: "Better an egg today than a chicken tomorrow."

Russia must be accounted for, so I called the Soviet Embassy and put it to them straight*: Is there anything behind the Iron Curtain* to equal "A bird in the hand is worth two in the bush"? Consternation[29] threaded its way* through the wires. Did they consider this just one more U.S. achievement to top?[30] And I could just imagine my entire conversation being properly recorded, translated, computed, and rushed to the decoding room.

[29] alarm, dismay

[30] do better than

An eternity[31] later, the clerk came back to ask me, "How you say cuckoo[32] in English?"

[31] a long time; time without end

[32] a type of small bird

Finally, she returned again with the information that "The cuckoo in hand is worth more than the crane[33] in the sky." She seemed relieved that she'd been able to come up with* an answer for me.

[33] a type of large bird

I am still puzzled by the Turkish Embassy. I talked with three different people there, ending with a gentleman who said, "*Yes*, we *do* have such a proverb!" There followed alternate periods of silence and hilarity[34] before he choked out, "I can't think of it!"

[34] loud and constant laughter

And thus a day of neighborly relations came to an end. ◆

Idioms and Phrases*

Embassy Row	*street where foreign embassies are located*
a bird in the hand is worth two in the bush	*don't risk what you have by trying to get what you don't have*
in common	*shared*
flying high	*very happy; overexcited*
came up against it	*faced a great difficulty*
verbal blast	*a strong, sudden rush of words*
in accord	*in agreement*
take your pick	*choose one*
chain of command	*different levels of authority in an organization, usually the military*
man (gentleman) of substance	*person of importance*
get to the bottom of	*find the truth*
give up	*stop trying*
put it to them straight	*told them directly*
Iron Curtain	*formerly, Eastern European Communist countries*
threaded its way	*passed through a small space*
come up with	*provide*

Post-Reading

Comprehension

1. Where does the narrator live?
2. What is her "quest"? Why does she begin it? What embassy does she first contact?
3. Name some of the embassies that she contacts and tell what happens when she contacts them.
4. What was one of the proverbs that did *not* involve birds?
5. Summarize what the narrator learns about the proverb "A bird in the hand is worth two in the bush" in different languages.

Responding to the Story

1. Which version of the proverb given in the story do you particularly like?
2. Does your language have a version of the proverb "A bird in the hand is worth two in the bush"? If so, how would it be translated into English?
3. The saying "A bird in the hand is worth two in the bush" is a common one and thus seems to reflect a common belief. Do you agree with this belief? Why or why not?
4. What is your impression of the narrator of the story? How would you describe her personality?
5. Does the different way each embassy answers show something about that country? If so, what is it?
6. In telling her story, the narrator assigns certain characteristics to each nationality. This is called *stereotyping.* What are some of the stereotypes that the narrator describes? What problems do you see with stereotypes like these?

VOCABULARY

Vocabulary Builder

Exercise 1

Give your opinion by answering yes or no to the following questions. Briefly explain your answers.

1. Was the narrator's *quest* worthwhile?
2. Were her actions *neighborly*?
3. Did the narrator actually talk to any *dignitaries*?
4. Did the narrator's questions cause *annoyance*?
5. Did most of the people the narrator spoke with treat her in a *courteous* manner?
6. Would you have felt *consternation* if the narrator had called you with her question?

Exercise 2

Pretend you are giving an embassy party. Answer yes *or* no *to each of the following questions. Give reasons for your answers.*

1. At an embassy party, when someone *jostles* you, do you spill your drink?
2. If there is no *substance* to your story, do people call you a liar?
3. If no one comes to your party, do you consider it a *debacle?*
4. If you speak *rapid-fire* English to a visiting Frenchman, will he understand you clearly?
5. Is it *prudent* to invite people who don't like each other to your party?
6. Are you better off inviting people who have something *in common?*
7. When someone tells you that *assuredly* he will come to your party, do you invite someone else instead?
8. If your guests are *gung-ho* for television, do you let them turn on the set?
9. Can you think of a better *diversion* for your party guests?
10. Do you do anything when the children at your party have the *giggles?*
11. Did an important *omission* from your guest list ever cause you embarrassment?

Dictionary Exercise

Study your dictionary and then describe, in your own words, the following terms.

1. backyard ______________________________
2. mansion ______________________________
3. fortune cookie ______________________________
4. bumpers ______________________________
5. pneumatic drill ______________________________

Idiom Exercise

Answer the questions.

1. If you were the narrator, would you have reacted to the *verbal blast* by *giving up*?
2. What interesting saying could you *come up with* for your classmates to translate into their languages?
3. What puzzle about English would you like to *get to the bottom of*?
4. Are you *in accord* with the idea that proverbs accurately reflect the way people think and act?

People and Languages

Do you know the terms for the people and languages of the countries mentioned in the story? (Some of the terms are mentioned; others are not.)

Fill in the person and language for each of the countries listed. Give the noun form, not adjective form, for the person (i.e., you should be able to put a(n) before each of the terms you use). Where a country has more than one language, you need to list only one. For example, a person who lives in Spain *is a* Spaniard, *and the language he or she speaks is* Spanish.

	Person	**Language**
1. Spain	*Spaniard*	*Spanish*
2. China	______	______
3. France	______	______
4. Iraq	______	______
5. Sweden	______	______
6. Norway	______	______
7. Denmark	______	______
8. Greece	______	______

9. Nepal ________________ ________________
10. Germany ________________ ________________
11. Russia ________________ ________________
12. Japan ________________ ________________
13. Italy ________________ ________________
14. Ireland ________________ ________________
15. Turkey ________________ ________________
16. Poland ________________ ________________
17. Mexico ________________ ________________
18. Israel ________________ ________________
19. Holland ________________ ________________

STRUCTURE

Who and Whom

Use who *when the pronoun is used as a subject; use* whom *when the pronoun is used as an object.*

Fill in the blanks with who *or* whom. *Use* whom *in places where either would be acceptable in spoken English.*

EXAMPLES: My car locked bumpers with that of a Far Eastern gentleman ____*who*____ was racing for the same parking place.

____*Whom*____ did Ms. Messmer call?

1. I explained my mission to the first woman ________________answered.
2. She asked, "________________ is this?"
3. Then she asked, "________________ are you with?"
4. She didn't know ________________ I should talk to.
5. She didn't know ________________ could answer my question.
6. I asked the young lady ________________ answered exactly what that meant.
7. I managed to convince her that I wasn't some gung-ho ornithologist ________________ was flying high.

(Continued on next page)

8. She deposited the problem in the lap of a pleasant, cordial gentleman ________________ sounded as though this might be the brightest spot in his day.
9. The woman to ________________ I addressed my question was extremely excitable.
10. I felt sorry for the poor man ________________ I talked with at the Italian embassy.
11. At the Turkish embassy, I talked with a gentleman ________________ said, "Yes, we do have such a proverb."

Proverbs and the Simple Present Tense

Exercise 1

Look over the following list of proverbs. Discuss with your classmates any proverbs whose meanings aren't clear. Notice that the proverbs use the simple present.

1. Too many cooks spoil the broth.
2. Birds of a feather flock together.
3. A penny saved is a penny earned.
4. Time and tide wait for no man.
5. People in glass houses shouldn't throw stones.
6. A fool and his money are soon parted.
7. An ounce of prevention is worth a pound of cure.
8. The early bird catches the worm.
9. Familiarity breeds contempt.
10. You can catch more flies with honey than with vinegar.
11. You can't judge a book by its cover.
12. Do not count your chickens until they are hatched.
13. Do not put all your eggs in one basket.
14. Strike while the iron is hot.

Exercise 2

What proverbs in your native language have meanings similar to the proverbs above? Give the equivalent proverb in your own language for as many of the proverbs as possible. Translate these equivalent proverbs into English. Be sure to use the simple present (or the imperative, if the proverb is phrased as a command). When you are finished, discuss with your classmates the various equivalent proverbs.

Comparatives

Make each string of words into a sentence by comparing the two things that can be compared. In each case say that the first thing mentioned has more of the quality mentioned than the second.

EXAMPLES: a bird in the hand/is good/two birds in the bush
A bird in the hand is better than two birds in the bush.

1. a trout in the hand/is good/a salmon in the pool
2. to have a thing in your hand/is good/to wait for two things
3. two birds in the bush/are bad/a bird in the hand
4. tempers in Scandinavia/are cool/tempers in France
5. the woman at the Spanish embassy/was friendly/the woman at the French embassy
6. the help the narrator received from the Turkish embassy/was little/the help she received from the Nepalese embassy
7. the response from the Turkish embassy/was puzzling/the responses from the other embassies
8. the Italian embassy/was noisy/the other embassies
9. the response from the Soviet embassy/took long/the responses from the other embassies

Follow Up

Topics for Discussion

1. In your opinion, to what extent do proverbs tend to be true? Look again at the proverbs on page 90. (a.) Are there some you feel are especially useful? Tell which ones and explain why. (b.) Are there some you disagree with? Tell which ones and explain why.
2. As a class, choose a proverb from the list and find out how it compares to "A bird in the hand. . . ." (a.) Does it occur in all the languages represented in the class? (b.) Are the translations more similar to one another, or more different from another, than those of "A bird in the hand. . . "?
3. Do you feel that the kinds of simplified descriptions of people from different countries that the narrator used encourage prejudice? Do they have another kind of effect, or do you feel they do not affect people's thinking? Explain your answer.

(Continued on next page)

4. The narrator did not know how to meet many foreigners in Washington. Where you live, if someone who is not foreign wants to meet foreigners, would it be difficult? How could they go about it?
5. Have you ever worked on research projects? If so, how did you get your information? Did your methods, like the narrator's, involve telephone calls? How difficult was it to get the information that you needed?

Topics for Writing

1. The authors of most proverbs are unknown. Some come from works of literature by such famous authors as Shakespeare or Aesop. Make up and write down your own proverbs on the subjects of sleep, food, and friendship.
2. Write a short story in which you show that a particular proverb is not true. For example, the proverb, "The apple does not fall far from the tree" is not always true. Don't some children grow up to be better than or different from their parents?
3. Sometimes different proverbs have conflicting messages. Write a paragraph in which you compare and contrast two such proverbs (English proverbs or English translations of proverbs from your language). Discuss, for example, how their subject matter is similar and how their advice is different.
4. When talking on the telephone with someone you didn't know, have you ever had an unexpectedly friendly encounter? Or have you ever unexpectedly received a verbal blast? Write two paragraphs about a surprising telephone conversation you have had.
5. What would happen to a person who was always quoting proverbs? Would other people find this person wise? dull? very annoying? Write a short story about a fictional person who always quotes proverbs and tell what happens to the person. (Use some of the proverbs on page 90 in your story, as well as any other real or made-up proverbs.)
6. What are some other proverbs in English? As a small research project, find out some other proverbs. Consult reference books and/or ask native speakers of English. Write several paragraphs describing the results of your research—the proverbs, their meanings, the existence of similar proverbs in your language, and conclusions, if you reach any, about proverbs in English.

UNIT 8

You Were Perfectly Fine

—DOROTHY PARKER

About the Author

Dorothy Parker *(1893–1967) was an American journalist and short-story writer, in addition to being the author of a best-selling book of light verse. Many of her poems and light sketches first appeared in* The New Yorker. *Her books include* Enough Rope *(1926) and* Not So Deep a Well *(1933). Parker is closely associated with the Jazz Age, which coincided approximately with the 1920s and was characterized by prosperity, jazz music, drinking, and partying. Many of her expressions and idioms come from that period when everyone was supposed to be carefree and gay and very clever. The humor in the following story is not always apparent, for the writer uses irony to make her point—everything she says is meant to be read in another way. Thus "you were perfectly fine" really means "you were awful." Read the story for such ironic meanings. Some of the idioms and slang expressions in the following story are now somewhat dated, although many are still used.*

◆ Previewing the Story

Look at the picture, the title, and the first paragraph of the story. Answer the questions, explaining each answer.

1. In what time period does the story take place? What details in the picture help you figure this out?
2. What mood does the man seem to be in? the woman? What do you think is the relationship between the man and the woman?
3. Have you ever told someone that he or she was "perfectly fine"? What did you mean?

◆ Thinking about the Topic

Think about and answer the following questions.

1. How do people often act after they have had too much alcohol to drink? How might he or she feel the next day?
2. In your country, how do you deal with people who tend to drink too much?

The pale young man eased[1] himself carefully into the low chair, and rolled his head to the side, so that the cool chintz[2] comforted his cheek and temple.[3]

"Oh, dear," he said. "Oh, dear, oh, dear, oh, dear. Oh."

The clear-eyed girl, sitting light and erect[4] on the couch, smiled brightly at him.

"Not feeling so well today?" she said.

"Oh, I'm great," he said. "Corking,[5] I am. Know what time I got up? Four o'clock this afternoon, sharp. I kept trying to make it, and every time I took my head off the pillow, it would roll under the bed. This isn't my head I've got on now. I think this is something that used to belong to Walt Whitman.[6] Oh, dear, oh, dear, oh, dear."

"Do you think maybe a drink would make you feel better?" she said.

"The hair of the mastiff that bit me*?" he said. "Oh, no, thank you. Please never speak of anything like that again. I'm through. I'm all, all through. Look at that hand; steady as a hummingbird.[7] Tell me, was I very terrible last night?"

"Oh, goodness," she said, "everybody was feeling pretty high.[8] You were all right."

"Yeah," he said. "I must have been dandy.[9] Is everybody sore[10] at me?"

"Good heavens, no," she said. "Everyone thought you were terribly funny. Of course, Jim Pierson was a little stuffy[11] there, for a minute at dinner. But people sort of held him back in his chair, and got him calmed down. I don't think anybody at the other tables noticed at all. Hardly anybody."

"He was going to sock[12] me?" he said. "Oh, Lord. What did I do to him?"

"Why, you didn't do a thing," she said. "You were perfectly fine. But you know how silly Jim gets, when he thinks anybody is making too much fuss over Elinor."

"Was I making a pass at* Elinor?" he said. "Did I do that?"

"Of course you didn't," she said. "You were only fooling,[13] that's all. She thought you were awfully amusing. She was having a marvelous time. She only got a little tiny bit annoyed[14] just once, when you poured the clam-juice down her back."

[1] moved slowly
[2] a glazed cotton material
[3] side of the forehead
[4] upright
[5] very good, excellent
[6] famous nineteenth-century American poet
[7] bird that makes a humming noise by the constant motion of its wings
[8] drunk
[9] wonderful
[10] angry
[11] old-fashioned
[12] strike with force
[13] joking
[14] angry

[15] part of the spinal column

[16] aristocratic family in Massachusetts

"My God," he said. "Clam-juice down her back. And every vertebra[15] a little Cabot.[16] Dear God. What'll I ever do?"

"Oh, she'll be all right," she said. "Just send her some flowers, or something. Don't worry about it. It isn't anything."

"No, I won't worry," he said. "I haven't got a care* in the world. I'm sitting pretty.* Oh, dear, oh, dear. Did I do any other fascinating tricks at dinner?"

"You were fine," she said. "Don't be so foolish about it. Everybody was crazy about you. The maître d'hôtel was a little worried because you wouldn't stop singing, but he really didn't mind. All he said was, he was afraid they'd close the place again, if there was so much noise. But he didn't care a bit, himself. I think he loved seeing you have such a good time. Oh, you were just singing away, there, for about an hour. It wasn't so terribly loud, at all."

[17] a delight, something that gives great pleasure

"So I sang," he said. "That must have been a treat.[17] I sang."

"Don't you remember?" she said. "You just sang one song after another. Everybody in the place was listening. They loved it. Only you kept insisting that you wanted to sing some song about some kind of fusiliers[18] or other, and everybody kept shushing you, and you'd keep trying to start it again. You were wonderful. We were all trying to make you stop singing for a minute, and eat something, but you wouldn't hear of it.* My, you were funny."

[18] old-fashioned soldiers

"Didn't I eat dinner?" he said.

"Oh, not a thing," she said. "Every time the waiter would offer you something, you'd give it right back to him, because you said that he was your long-lost brother, changed in the cradle[19] by a gypsy band,[20] and that anything you had was his. You had him simply roaring[21] at you."

[19] infant's bed

[20] group

[21] laughing or shouting loudly

[22] very great

"I bet I did," he said. "I bet I was comical. Society's Pet. I must have been. And what happened then, after my overwhelming[22] success with the waiter?"

"Why, nothing much," she said. "You took a sort of dislike to some old man with white hair, sitting across the room, because you didn't like his necktie and you wanted to tell him about it. But we got you out, before he got really mad."

"Oh, we got out," he said. "Did I walk?"

"Walk! Of course you did," she said. "You were absolutely all right. There was that nasty[23] stretch[24] of ice on the sidewalk, and you did sit down awfully hard, you poor dear. But good heavens, that might have happened to anybody."

[23] unpleasant

[24] piece, unbroken length

"Oh, sure," he said. "Louisa Alcott[25] or anybody. So I fell down on the sidewalk. That would explain what's the matter with my—Yes. I see. And then what, if you don't mind?"

[25] famous author of children's books

"Ah, now, Peter!" she said. "You can't sit there and say you don't remember what happened after that! I did think that maybe you were just a little tight[26] at dinner—oh, you were perfectly all right, and all that, but I did know you were feeling pretty gay. But you were so serious, from the time you fell down—I never knew you to be that way. Don't you know, how you told me I had never seen your real self before? Oh, Peter, I just couldn't bear it, if you didn't remember that lovely long ride we took together in the taxi! Please, you do remember that, don't you? I think it would simply kill me, if you didn't."

[26] drunk

"Oh, yes," he said. "Riding in the taxi. Oh, yes, sure. Pretty long ride, hmm?"

"Round and round and round the park," she said. "Oh, and the trees were shining so in the moonlight. And you said you never knew before that you really had a soul."

"Yes," he said. "I said that. That was me."

"You said such lovely, lovely things," she said. "And I'd never known, all this time, how you had been feeling about me, and I'd never dared to let you see how I felt about you. And then last night—oh, Peter dear, I think that taxi ride was the most important thing that ever happened to us in our lives."

"Yes," he said. "I guess it must have been."

"And we're going to be so happy," she said. "Oh, I just want to tell everybody! But I don't know—I think maybe it would be sweeter to keep it all to ourselves."*

"I think it would be," he said.

"Isn't it lovely?" she said.

"Yes," he said. "Great."

"Lovely!" she said.

"Look here," he said, "do you mind if I have a drink? I mean, just medicinally[27] you know. I'm off the stuff* for life, so help me. But I think I feel a collapse[28] coming on."

[27] for reasons of health

[28] breakdown, loss of physical strength

"Oh, I think it would do you good," she said. "You poor boy, it's a shame you feel so awful. I'll go make you a whiskey and soda."

"Honestly," he said, "I don't see how you could ever want to speak to me again, after I made such a fool of myself, last night. I think I'd better go join a monastery[29] in Tibet."

[29] an isolated religious home for Buddhists, here suggesting a place that is very far away from the world

"You crazy idiot!" she said. "As if I could ever let you go away now! Stop talking like that. You were perfectly fine."

She jumped up from the couch, kissed him quickly on the forehead, and ran out of the room.

The pale young man looked after her and shook his head long and slowly, then dropped it in his damp and trembling hands.

"Oh, dear," he said. "Oh, dear, oh, dear, oh, dear." ◆

Idioms and Phrases*

the hair of the mastiff (dog) that bit me	*meaning here the same thing that hurt me*
making a pass at	*flirting with*
not have a care in the world	*not have any worries*
I'm sitting pretty	*all is well with me*
hear of it	*allow or consider it*
keep it all to ourselves	*keep it secret*
off the stuff	*doing without it*

Post-Reading

Comprehension

1. Was Peter really "perfectly fine"? Why or why not?
2. Why didn't Peter remember anything about the previous evening?
3. Why didn't Peter eat anything in the restaurant?
4. Why was Jim Pierson angry with Peter?
5. What other outrageous things did Peter do while he was drunk?
6. What did Peter do after leaving the restaurant?
7. On learning what he had done, how did Peter feel? How can you tell?
8. Did Peter really want to marry the girl? How do you know?

Responding to the Story

1. From their conversation, do you think Peter's girlfriend had a clear picture of his character? How can you tell?
2. What attitude does Peter's girlfriend say that the other people in the restaurant had toward his behavior? Can her description of their reactions be trusted?

3. What attitudes does she seem to have toward his behavior? What does she seem to think of him?
4. What social class do these people belong to? What kind of lifestyle is the author describing?
5. What do you think Peter's feelings toward the girl are? Give a reason for your answer.
6. Why does Peter's girlfriend insist that he was "perfectly fine"?
7. What do you think happens after the scene described? Does Peter "get off the stuff"? Do his friends still talk to him? Does he marry the girl? Does he leave town? Explain why you think as you do.

VOCABULARY

Vocabulary Builder

Fill in the blanks with the following words.

care	annoyed
collapse	silly
ease	stretch
erect	fooling
nasty	temples
overwhelming	treat

1. Because his head and body ached so much, Peter slumped over in his chair and couldn't sit ____________________.
2. The headache was especially bad; there was a pounding in his ____________________.
3. Jim Pierson acted ____________________, as he always did when he thought Peter was making a fuss over Elinor.
4. It's unlikely that the other customers in the restaurant considered Peter's singing much of a ____________________.
5. Although Peter's girlfriend thought that he was only ____________________, everyone else was ____________________ with him.
6. Peter fell while walking on a ____________________ of ice.
7. As a result of the fall, he had a ____________________ bruise that made it difficult for him to sit down.
8. As he learned what he had done the previous evening, Peter fell into a state of ____________________ despair.
9. Peter could not ____________________ himself out of this difficult situation.
10. He was so shaken that he felt like he was about to ____________________ —or at least like he needed a drink.
11. Although Peter felt bad, the girl acted like she no longer had a ____________________ in the world.

Idiom Exercise

Exercise 1

Tell whether each statement is true or false.

1. If you are sitting pretty, you don't have any worries.
2. When everyone asked Peter to stop singing, he wouldn't hear of it.
3. Peter said, "Let's keep it to ourselves," so his girlfriend told everyone about their engagement.
4. When Jim saw Peter making a pass at Elinor, he wasn't jealous at all.

Exercise 2

Make up your own sentences using each of the idioms above.

1. ______________________________
2. ______________________________
3. ______________________________
4. ______________________________

Word Forms

Fill in the blanks with the correct forms of the words listed.

1. ease, easy, easing, easily
   a. The young man was ______________ himself into the chair when she walked into the room.
   b. I can complete this paper ______________.
   c. He was trying to ______________ himself out of the embarrassing situation.
   d. Peter thought it would be ______________ to stand up until he tried to do it.
2. comfort, comforted, comforting, comfortable
   a. It is ______________ to know that there is someone who cares.
   b. Peter enjoyed the ______________ of his apartment.
   c. This morning, even in the low chair, he couldn't make himself ______________.
   d. The young woman ______________ him by saying, "You were perfectly fine."
3. insist, insisting, insistence, insistent
   a. His ______________ on singing in the restaurant made him unpopular with the people at the other tables.
   b. His ______________ remarks about the man's necktie began to annoy the people at his own table.
   c. Why did you ______________ on coming to this restaurant?
   d. I don't understand why she keeps ______________ that he have a drink.

4. amusing, amusingly, amusement, unamused
   a. Peter was the main source of ____________________ at last night's party.
   b. He was ____________________ affectionate toward Elinor.
   c. Jim seemed ____________________ by Peter's behavior.
   d. Falling on the ice can't have been very ____________________.

STRUCTURE

Interjections

The speech in the story starts and ends with an interjection, "Oh, dear." **Interjections** are words or phrases that are used in exclamations; they express emotion but don't really add to the meaning of what is being said.

Exercise 1

Both of the characters use many interjections. Find some of these interjections and write them next to the appropriate character.

EXAMPLE: the girl: oh, goodness; good heavens; . . .

1. Peter: ____
2. the girl: ____

Exercise 2

Can you explain why these characters use so many interjections? What are some similar interjections in your language? How would they be said in English?

Adverbs Modifying Adjectives

In the title "You Were Perfectly Fine," the adjective *fine* is modified by the adverb *perfectly.* Adverbs modifying adjectives often add emphasis or indicate degree.

Exercise 1

Look through the story for other examples of adverbs modifying adjectives—there are many other examples—and list these examples. Look over your list. Why are there so many of these adverbs? Which character uses them? What purpose do they seem to serve?

EXAMPLE: pretty high
terribly funny
. . .

Exercise 2

ROLE PLAY: With a partner, write and then role-play a situation in which one person is giving another person some bad news. The person who is giving the bad news should try to tell the news in a way that makes it sound not quite so bad. Adverb + adjective structures should be used for this purpose. The story can be humorous, like "You Were Perfectly Fine," or it can be serious.

Short Answers

In spoken English, questions are often answered with sentences that are grammatically incomplete—that is, they may be missing the subject, verb, and/or other parts of a grammatical sentence.

EXAMPLES: 1. "Was I very terrible?" he asked.
"You were not at all terrible," she answered. —>
"Not at all," she answered.

2. "Not feeling so well today?" she said.
"Oh, I'm feeling great," he said. —>
"Great," he said.

3. "Did I make a pass at Elinor?" he said.
"Of course you didn't make a pass at Elinor," she said. —>
"Of course you didn't," she said.

Exercise 1

Find and list some other shortened—grammatically incomplete—forms in the dialogue in the story. (Hint: You can start by looking at the questions above.)

Exercise 2

How common are these incomplete forms in spoken English? Record several minutes of spoken English—from television, radio, and/or conversations—and listen carefully to hear whether such forms are used. Write down any of these sentences that you hear.

Punctuation

Insert commas, periods, and semicolons where necessary in the following sentences.

EXAMPLES: 1. Because I was very thirsty, I drank some water.

2. I drank some water because I was very thirsty.

3. I drank some water. I was very thirsty.

1. The maître d'hôtel was a little worried because Peter wouldn't stop singing but he really didn't mind
2. People when they drink too much whiskey do foolish things

3. "Just send her some flowers and she'll be all right" he said
4. Peter a character in the story seems very confused
5. Peter is a character in this story he seems very confused
6. The girl described his drinking singing laughing and falling
7. In the morning I thought I had lost my head however I found it under the bed
8. The song he sang made everyone laugh even though no one understood it
9. "Look at me" he said "My hands are trembling"

Follow Up

Topics for Discussion

1. In addition to Peter's problems, what other sorts of problems can result from excessive drinking?
2. Based on the story, what do you think of the lifestyle of Peter and his friends? Would you want to be part of this group? Why or why not?
3. Have you ever been in a public place where someone—because of drunkenness or for some other reason—started misbehaving? What happened?
4. ***Role Play:*** With a classmate, act out what occurred between Peter and the older man when Peter told him he didn't like his tie.
5. What are some of the reasons why people drink excessively? When are people most likely to drink excessively?
6. Why do people forget what they did when they were drunk?
7. If you were Peter's friend, how much would you tell him about his activities while he was drunk?
8. ***Role Play:*** Pretend you are trying to convince a friend who has had too much to drink not to drive his or her car home. In pairs, act out the scene.
9. Do you think that drinking is a major problem in the United States? in your country? Explain.

Topics for Writing

1. Describe the thoughts running through Peter's mind as the woman told him about his actions of the previous evening. Write as if you were Peter.
2. In a small group, write a dialogue of the conversation that might have occurred between Peter, Elinor, and Jim Pierson—either that evening or the next time that Peter sees Elinor and Jim.
3. Write a brief continuation of the story, in which you clarify what happens with Peter and the girl. The scene you write can take place when the girl comes back into the room or it can take place at some later time.
4. Write a short story about a couple who are on a date in a restaurant. Make sure to include a great deal of dialogue.
5. In an essay of three or more paragraphs, compare your social activities with Peter's.

UNIT 9

Harpist on Horseback

—HILDA COLE ESPY

About the Author

Hilda Cole Espy *is both a writer and a housewife. She lives in Mount Kisco, New York, with her family. This story about Cassie and her harp is based on Espy's true-life experiences in Mount Kisco, which are described in her book* Quiet, Yelled Mrs. Rabbit *(1958).*

◆ Previewing the Story

Look at the picture, the title, and the first paragraph of the story. Answer the questions, explaining each answer.

1. Why is the harpist on horseback up in the clouds?
2. Describe the kind of person that you think Cassie, the girl in the picture, might be.
3. What do you think this story will be about?

◆ Thinking about the Topic

Think about and answer the following questions.

1. Have you ever had an unusual ambition? What was it?
2. Do you ever daydream about doing impossible things? What kinds of things?
3. What kind of music do you associate with the harp?
4. In your country, what might be considered a popular musical instrument? Why do you think it is popular?

Cassie was eight the first time she mentioned that she wanted to play the harp.[1] Now and then she still jumped off her bed to see if she could fly like Peter Pan.[2] Her bedroom floor being uncarpeted, we usually knew when she had once again met with disillusionment.[3]

Her three older sisters were turning young-ladyish and making sense at that time. But Cassie was a character[4] who, whether she could fly or not, still managed to spend most of her time in never-never land.* Her rainy-day drawings were of frowzy[5] little mermaids° and frowzy little fairies[6] who bore a strong resemblance* to the artist. Cassie seldom combed her reddish-brown hair or tied her shoelaces or washed her neck.

In those days she was a genius at the irrelevant[7] question. I recall her asking one lovely sunny May day, "Mommy, do you think it'll rain next Halloween?"[8] She had many "ideers"[9] as she called them, and they were all so fantastic that it took heroic restraint[10] to deal with them patiently. While her big sisters might ask on a Saturday morning if they could walk downtown and buy some bobby pins,[11] Cassie would ask if she could catch the next train to New York, some fifty miles from our village of Mount Kisco, and buy a horse.

One Saturday morning we were sitting around the kitchen table. Mona, Freddy, and Joanna were discussing what they'd like to be when they grew up. Mona thought she'd like to be a vet,[12] Freddy planned to design clothes, and Joanna decided to get married and have a lot of children. Cassie had been swiveling[13] her head around thoughtfully.

"Mommy," she chirped, "do you think I could combine riding horseback with playing the harp?"

We all fastened mirthfully[14] disparaging[15] gazes upon her. "Let's not be weird,"[16] I teased.[17] "Let's have no member of this family cantering[18] about while playing the harp. . . ."

Cassie glared.[19] Then her eyes filled with tears.

"That's not what I meant!" she shouted. "I didn't mean I'd play it *on* the horse!"

And she went running upstairs to her room, letting out loud boohoos. When I followed to make up* with her, she cried, "You think

[1] stringed musical instrument

[2] imaginary character in a children's story

[3] disappointment

[4] unusual or original person

[5] dirty; untidy

[6] imaginary beings with magic powers

[7] unconnected with what is being discussed

[8] holiday in October

[9] ideas

[10] control

[11] hairpins

mermaid

[12] veterinarian; animal doctor

[13] turning

[14] merrily

[15] belittling

[16] strange

[17] said jokingly

[18] galloping on a horse

[19] stared angrily

[20] want to
[21] going to
[22] moved forward suddenly
[23] untidy

everything I say is funny! I wanna[20] play the harp and I'm *gonna*[21] play the harp!" She darted[22] her disheveled[23] head at me like a small snake.

I patted her bony little shoulder. This "ideer," like the "ideer" of buying a horse, would pass, I knew. (I thought I knew!)

[24] handsome actor

In the next six months Cassie gave up attempting to fly like Peter Pan and stopped saying that she was going to marry Mel Ferrer.[24] But she did not stop predicting that she was going to play the harp. She managed ingeniously[25] to insinuate[26] her yen[27] for the instrument into all family conversations. If Mona complained of poison ivy,[28] Cassie would remark that she was glad *she* didn't get poison ivy, as it might interfere with her playing the harp. Let Joanna mention that she'd like ice skates for Christmas, and Cassie would smile and crowd winsomely[29] up against her father or me and croon,[30] "I know what I'd like for Christmas."

[25] cleverly
[26] suggest, hint
[27] desire
[28] an itchy rash caused by the poison ivy plant
[29] lovably
[30] hum gently

That September, when the three older girls resumed piano lessons, Cassie was offered a chance to join them. She angrily refused. "You know what I want to play," she said.

I felt it was time for a showdown.[31] "All right, we'll go see Mr. Stochek," I said. "We'll find out how to get hold of* a harp."

[31] an event that forces a situation to its conclusion

Mr. Stochek sells violins, tubas, harmonicas, oboes, guitars, clarinets in Mount Kisco. He also arranges for a child to take lessons on any instrument he elects.[32]

[32] chooses

"Mr. Stochek," I said as we entered the store, "this is Cassie. She wants to take harp lessons."

"Harp lessons?" He made a why-can't-anything-go-right-today sort of face. "Why do you want to take harp lessons?"

Cassie glared at him.

"I just do," she said.

"Want to buy a harp, do you, Mrs. Espy?" he asked me dryly.[33] "Cost you twenty-five hundred dollars."

[33] sarcastically; humorously

"Of course not. Even if we had that much money, which we don't, we wouldn't want to *buy* a harp without knowing how much talent Cassie has or how hard she is willing to work."

Mr. Stochek began to shake his head.

"I don't know where you'd ever rent a harp," he said. "Even if you found one to rent, where would you find a harp teacher around here?"

I looked at Cassie. "See?" said my look. "Why don't you learn to play an instrument you could use in the school band?"[34] Mr. Stochek challenged Cassie. "You could march in all the parades," he suggested. "A harp's very, very hard to learn."

He reached into the glass display case where instruments flashed and glowed. "See this here, Cassie? This is an oboe. Listen to this. . . ."

He put the instrument to his lips and produced a rich oriental-sounding series of notes. Cassie stared stubbornly, refusing to be charmed.

Mr. Stochek strummed a guitar and sang a few bars of "Davy Crockett." He blew a trumpet. He played "Dark Eyes" on an accordion.

"You like that?" he'd ask Cassie after each performance.

"It's all right," she'd say, with maddening[35] listlessness,[36] "but I don't *want* to play anything until I play the harp."

Mr. Stochek sagged[37] against the counter.[38]

"Thank you," I said.

"You're welcome." His voice was very carefully controlled.

I walked Cassie out on Main Street; her eyes were spilling over with tears, and she had her mouth stuck out like a Ubangi.[39]

"Now listen, Cassie," I said. "If you want to play something, you'll just have to play something that's available, that's all."

The tears rolled on.

"How can you take harp lessons if we can't get hold of a harp?" I screamed.

She marched along silently, tragically.

"Stop drizzling!"[40] I cried. "We tried—what more can we do?"

"I'll pray," declared Cassie. "I'll pray every night."

The following spring I made one of my rare trips to New York to lunch with a friend. Before catching the 3:20 home I decided to walk across 57th Street and window-shop[41] on my way to Grand Central Station. I thought this route was my own idea, but of course Cassie had been constantly in touch* with Heaven, and they're all harpists up there except for the horn player, Gabriel. Suddenly I saw a neat black sign: "Lyon and Healy. Harps."

Cassie's face came to mind, the big gray eyes, the face drawn[42] with wistfulness.[43] As in a dream I found my way upstairs to a quiet room, gleaming[44] with huge golden harps. A man was sitting at a desk at the end of an aisle formed by harps.

[34] group of persons playing music together

[35] annoying

[36] lack of energy or interest

[37] leaned tiredly

[38] table in a store

[39] member of an African tribe known for stretching the lower lip as a sign of beauty

[40] crying; lightly raining

[41] look in store windows

[42] tight with worry

[43] unsatisfied desire

[44] shining

"I am Mark Hunzinger. What can I do for you?" he inquired cordially.[45]

"I have a little girl, Cassie," I began. "She gets queer[46] ideas. Now she wants to play the harp."

"Tell me about her," he invited. "How long has she had this idea?"

"For a couple of years," I said, twisting my gloves. "She keeps saying she wants to play one. She keeps saying she *hears* harps—in orchestrations and things."

"Well, she's beginning to sound like a real harpist!" pronounced Mr. Hunzinger. He spoke like a doctor diagnosing the mumps.[47]

"Most harpists, like Cassie, have had to overcome[48] a lot of resistance," he said. "It's not the easiest instrument to get hold of and it's difficult to play. Did *you* ever, by any chance, want to play the harp?"

"Oh no," I said. "It never would have occurred[49] to me."

It seemed important to him to establish that this was Cassie's own burning idea, that she was not the daughter of a frustrated[50] harpist.

"She certainly should have her harp," he decided briskly. "I'll rent you one." He put his hand on a beautiful little harp, crowned like a queen. "This would be the right size for Cassie."

I gulped.[51]

"Don't you think perhaps we'd better think about it?" I asked. Renting the harp was expensive. Somehow I felt I hadn't communicated to Mr. Hunzinger what Cassie was really like, wanting to fly off her bed and marry Mel Ferrer.

"This is a difficult instrument and the sooner she starts the better," he said. "You can pick it up Friday, on the loading platform at Steinway Hall. And meantime, you call Lucile Lawrence, in Larchmont. She teaches the harp. I'll tell Miss Lawrence all about Cassie, and I think she'll try to arrange to teach her."

Homeward bound on a later train, it seemed to me that my life was already strewn[52] with abandoned[53] fancies of the children: unfinished knitting, puppies who were now dogs, kittens who were now cats, drum majors' batons,[54] and oil painting sets . . . and now it seemed I had a great big harp on my hands.

My husband and I drove the station wagon into New York on Friday night to pick up the harp. In its large wooden case it occupied the entire car except for the front seat; it required the combined muscles of my

[45] warmly, sincerely
[46] strange, unusual
[47] a childhood disease
[48] get over, get beyond
[49] come (to mind)
[50] unfulfilled; disappointed
[51] swallowed quickly
[52] scattered
[53] given up
[54] sticks used by leaders of marching bands

husband and Mr. Hunzinger to wedge it into place.* "She couldn't play the flute. Oh no," I said crossly.[55]

[55] irritably

Cassie was waiting up for us at home. She held the door open gravely while we grunted[56] and heaved[57] the heavy harp case into the living room. She did not jump up and down and clap her hands, as she usually did when she was pleased. She stood quietly while we lifted the harp out of the case. Then she ran one finger up and down the strings. A strange and beautiful sound went vibrating[58] through the house. She gave a sudden, radiant[59] smile.

[56] made deep sounds
[57] lifted
[58] echoing; shaking
[59] glowing

"It's just what I thought it would be like," she said.

That Sunday we drove Cassie to Larchmont for her first lesson with Miss Lawrence—one of the many, many Sundays we were to spend this way, an hour to Larchmont, an hour or more for the lesson itself, an hour back.

Propped up* on a telephone book on a bench behind Miss Lawrence's enormous concert grand harp, Cassie looked very small. I found myself afraid for her; I didn't want her to meet frustration.

Miss Lawrence showed her how to balance the harp and explained how a harpist, on playing a chord,[60] closes his hand and raises it, as if he had captured the sound in his palm.

[60] three or more notes sounded together

"Nijinsky, the dancer, worked all one summer in Maine with Salzedo, the harpist, to develop these motions, Cassie," she said. "An audience tends to watch a harpist. So it is important how we look."

Cassie scuffled[61] and hitched[62] reflectively. Why, I'll bet she starts tucking in her blouse, I thought. (She did. As she improved on the harp, she improved in neatness.)

[61] moved restlessly
[62] pulled quickly

I listened to Miss Lawrence outline the ground she expected Cassie to cover by next week: the notes of the scales, the functions of the seven pedals. "And, Cassie," she added, "would you write me a piece?"[63]

[63] musical composition

"All right," said Cassie, who had never read a note of music in her life, let alone write it!

She doesn't know Cassie, I thought apprehensively.[64] Cassie, the most disorganized member of the family, who had always preferred fantastic dreams to grappling[65] with realities within actual reach! But Miss Lawrence *did* know Cassie; it was I who did not know Cassie—the harpist.

[64] fearfully
[65] struggling

She learned her notes and she learned her pedals and she composed her piece, too, and Miss Lawrence made an arrangement of it for her. It was the first thing she played after "Yankee Doodle." (There is nothing quite like "Yankee Doodle" played smartly on a big harp by a small girl.)

But I still had reservations* about Cassie's future on the instrument. I wasn't a musician, but I had friends who were musicians, and I knew how hard they had to work. I watched and waited. And meantime learned a few things, like how to string a harp, and how to tune[66] a harp.

[66] adjust the strings of

When we planned our vacation on Cape Cod, I thought Cassie might be relieved to leave the harp behind, escape from practicing. But she wanted to take it with her.

"You see, I have more time to practice in the summer," she said.

Miss Lawrence backed her up,* and we arranged to transport the harp to Cape Cod.

When we returned to school that fall, Cassie had to make a decision she'll have to make over and over and over again as time goes on. Did she care enough about practicing the harp to forego[67] many of the activities in which her friends were engaging?

[67] do without

"I'd sorta[68] like to go in for* cheerleading,"[69] she said to me wistfully, "but I can't go out for cheerleading because then I wouldn't have enough time for my harp."

[68] sort of

[69] chanting and dancing in a group to encourage a team to win

I was on the point of thinking that Cassie would never again make my head spin with an impossible "ideer" when, one Saturday morning, I heard her ask her father to drive her to Sunnyfield Farm. They give horseback riding lessons there.

"Now just a minute!" I whirled from the sink. "We can't afford[70] riding lessons as well as harp lessons, Cassie!"

[70] have the money for

"I know that." She nodded. "I just want to *look* at the horses. . ."

On her return she happily reported that George, the riding master, had let her help him groom[71] the horses.

[71] clean and brush

"Some Saturdays, when the horses aren't all being ridden, he'll let me ride after I groom them," she said. "Wasn't that nice of George?"

My eyes narrowed. For suddenly I remembered her question, "Do you think I could combine horseback riding with playing the harp?"

I thought of calling George and warning him. But then I decided, George can learn his own lessons. I'm too busy figuring out how to buy the harp!

Most Sundays we drove Cassie to Larchmont for her lesson. It was never dull[72] to listen to Miss Lawrence teaching because she somehow taught much more than the harp.

[72] uninteresting

"You must look at good pictures, Cassie," she told our daughter, "and read good books. This will help you play the harp well."

"You must use *everything,* Cassie," Miss Lawrence would say. "You must listen with your ears as well as think with your mind and see with your eyes that read the music."

How true! Most of us don't use everything but lean[73] too hard on one faculty[74] or another . . . our great big brains, or our great big hearts. . . .

[73] depend

[74] sense; ability

In the fall of Cassie's thirteenth year, a little more than two years after her first trip to Miss Lawrence's, she joined the Westchester Youth Symphony in White Plains.

She got her audition[75] music (preludes from the opera *Carmen*) in the mail two days before she was due to play for Norman Leydon, the conductor. On Saturday morning her father and I lifted the harp into the station wagon and drove Cassie to the County Center Building at White Plains, for her audition.

[75] trial hearing

She made the orchestra and stayed for rehearsal. And now, every Saturday morning, we load the harp into the station wagon at 9:15 so that Cassie can be set up and on the stage at White Plains by 9:45. The orchestra rehearses until 12:30, and by one o'clock we're back in Mount Kisco again.

I've said it before and I'll say it again: Cassie had better marry a moving man. A moving man who is fond of* horses. ◆

IDIOMS AND PHRASES*

never-never land	*imaginary residence of Peter Pan*
bear a resemblance	*look similar to*
make up	*become friends again after a quarrel*
get hold of	*get possession of*
in touch	*talking or writing to*
wedge into place	*fit into a tight place*
propped up	*raised*
have reservation about	*have doubts about*
back up	*support, agree with*
go in for	*work at*
is fond of	*likes, has an affection for*

Post-Reading

Comprehension

1. How was Cassie "different"?
2. What were her two main interests?
3. What were some of the interests of Mrs. Espy's other children?
4. Where did Mrs. Espy find a harp?
5. What was Cassie's reaction when she saw her harp for the first time? Was that her usual reaction to something that pleased her?
6. How did the harp keep Cassie from doing other things with her friends?
7. Describe Cassie's harp lessons and her progress with the harp.
8. How did Cassie manage to go horseback riding even though her parents couldn't pay for riding lessons?

Responding to the Story

1. Do you think Cassie will ever get a horse? Why or why not?
2. How did the harp expand and improve Cassie's character?
3. What kind of adult do you think Cassie is going to grow up to be? Explain your answer.
4. Why do Cassie's two main interests seem "weird"?
5. What kind of person is Cassie's mother, Mrs. Espy?
6. What do you think would have happened if Mrs. Espy hadn't been able to get Cassie her harp?

Vocabulary

Vocabulary Builder

Exercise 1

Write sentences using the adverbs from the list.

Example: She ran her fingers *playfully* over the strings.

ingeniously	mirthfully	crossly
cordially	dryly	apprehensively

Exercise 2

Choose five adjectives from the list, and write a short paragraph using one of the adjectives in each sentence. Some of the words can be verb forms as well as adjectives; make sure that you use these words as adjectives.

EXAMPLE: Her hair was *disheveled* by the wind. Still, she ran through the *drizzling* rain. When she entered the room, her mother remarked on her *frowzy* appearance.

frowzy	radiant	dull
irrelevant	disparaging	maddening
disheveled	weird	abandoned

Idiom Exercise

Fill in the blanks with the following idioms. Change verb forms if necessary to fit the context of the sentence.

make up	back up
be in touch	get hold of
bear a resemblance	have reservations about

1. The mermaids and fairies in Cassie's drawings always ____________________ to Cassie.
2. Mr. Hunzinger told Mrs. Espy that he would ____________________ with Miss Lawrence to tell her about Cassie's interest in lessons.
3. Even when Cassie's harp lessons began in such a promising way, Mrs. Espy still ____________________ Cassie's going into music as a career.
4. At Mr. Stochek's store, children could ____________________ almost any instrument they wanted to play, but he did not have any harps.
5. Her mother tried very hard to ____________________ with Cassie after the quarrel.
6. In general, the Espys were supportive parents and ________________ their children's desires, even when these desires were unusual.

Word Forms

Fill in the blanks with the correct form of the words listed.

1. frustrate, frustrating, frustration
   a. If she wants to study the harp, do not ____________________ her.
   b. She felt great ____________________ at not being able to ride a horse.
   c. It is ____________________ to study for a test and then to fail it.
2. relevant, irrelevant, relevance
   a. As a child, Cassie had a tendency to make ____________________ remarks.
   b. Mr. Hunzinger felt it was ____________________ to find out whether Mrs. Espy was a frustrated harp player.
   c. According to Miss Lawrence, everything had some ____________________ to playing the harp.
3. disparage, disparaging, disparagingly, disparagement
   a. He treated her ____________________ in music class.
   b. Don't be ____________________ when someone plays less well than you.
   c. Don't ____________________ her good intentions to practice all day.
   d. The teacher's lecture to his students was full of ____________________.
4. apprehensive, apprehensively, apprehension
   a. Because she expected to be laughed at, Cassie looked at her mother with ____________________.
   b. Although she had done her homework, she walked to the blackboard ____________________.
   c. She is always ____________________ about performing before a large audience.

STRUCTURE

Would **(Future in the Past) and** ***Will*** **(Future in the Present)**

Would is used, instead of *will,* when talking about the future from the perspective of the past time, instead of from the perspective of the present time.

When the verb in one clause is in the present tense, use *will* in the other clause.

When the verb in one clause is in the past tense, use *would* in the other clause.

Complete the sentences with would *or* will.

EXAMPLES: If Nina complained of poison ivy, Cassie ___*would*___ remark that she was glad she didn't have it.

It's just what I thought it ___*would*___ be like.

I wonder if I ___*will*___ like my new horse.

1. Mrs. Espy thought that Cassie's ideas of playing the harp and riding horses ____________ pass.
2. It's only May, and Cassie wants to know if it ____________ rain next Halloween.
3. Mona, Freddy, and Joanna were sitting around the kitchen table and discussing what they ____________ be when they grew up.
4. Mrs. Espy was on the point of thinking that Cassie ____________ never again have an impossible idea when she heard her ask her father to take her to Sunnyfield Farm.
5. Some Saturdays, after Cassie grooms the horses, George ____________ let her ride them.
6. From now on, Cassie ____________ have to decide, again and again, whether to give things up in order to play the harp.
7. Mrs. Espy thinks that, when Cassie grows up, she ____________ have to find a very special person to marry.

Past Perfect and Future Perfect Tenses

The past perfect tense is used to talk about actions that have already happened at a given time in the past (see Unit 3). It is formed with *had* (the past form of the auxiliary verb *have*) plus the past participle of a verb; for example, *By the time Mr. and Mrs. Espy came home with the harp, Cassie's sisters* ***had*** *already* ***gone*** *to bed.* The future perfect, in contrast, is used to talk about actions that will be past at a given time in the future. It is formed with *will* plus *have* plus the past participle of a verb; for example, *By the time Mr. and Mrs. Espy come home, Cassie's sisters* ***will have*** *already* ***gone*** *to bed.*

Exercise 1

Complete the following sentences with the past perfect of the verbs indicated.

Example: By the time Cassie got her harp, she ___had given up___ (give up) saying that she wanted to marry Mel Ferrer.

1. When Cassie was still a small child, she ____________ (already/begin) to seem different from her sisters.
2. By the time Cassie was eight, she ____________ (already/decide) that she wanted to play the harp.
3. By the time Cassie was eleven, she ____________ (take) some harp lessons.
4. By the time she was thirteen, she ____________ (become) a member of a youth orchestra.
5. By then she also ____________ (learn) to groom a horse.

Exercise 2

What happens to Cassie after the age of thirteen? Write three sentences telling what happens to Cassie at later points in her life. In each sentence use the future perfect and a time expression (e.g., By the time she is . . . , When she is . . .).

Example: By the time she is married, she will have performed many solos.

1. ____
2. ____
3. ____

Exercise 3

What had you done by certain times in the past? What will you have done by certain points of time in the future? Write three sentences using the past perfect and three sentences using the future perfect. Use a time expression in each sentence to indicate the point of time you are talking about.

1. ______________________________
2. ______________________________
3. ______________________________
4. ______________________________
5. ______________________________
6. ______________________________

Real and Unreal Conditionals

Conditional sentences have an *if* clause and a result clause. They can be real (possible), or unreal (contrary to fact). Conditionals about the future, if real, are formed with a present tense verb in the *if* clause and *will* in the result clause; if unreal, they are formed with a past tense verb in the *if* clause and *would* in the result clause. For example, *If Cassie has the desire, she will learn to play the harp* is a real conditional, and *If Cassie had the desire, she would learn to play the oboe* is an unreal conditional.

Exercise 1

Complete each sentence by filling in the correct form of the verb and by filling in will *or* would.

EXAMPLE: If Cassie ____*does*____ (do) well at the audition, she ____*will*____ make the orchestra.

1. If Cassie ____________ (be) able to fly, her family ____________ not hear the thumps on the uncarpeted bedroom floor.
2. Even if she ____________ (have) enough money, which she doesn't, Cassie's mother ____________ not want to buy a harp without knowing how much talent Cassie has.

(Continued on next page)

3. Mr. Stochek doesn't rent harps, and even if he ________________ (rent) harps, Cassie ________________ have a hard time finding a teacher.

4. If Mrs. Espy ________________ (be) willing to rent a harp for Cassie, Mr. Hunzinger ________________ rent her one immediately.

5. According to Mr. Hunzinger, if Cassie ________________ (want) to learn the harp, Miss Lawrence ________________ teach her.

6. Cassie decided not to go out for cheerleading because, if she ________________ (go out) for cheerleading, she ________________ not have enough time to practice the harp.

7. If her family ________________ (have) more money than they do, perhaps Cassie ________________ take both harp and riding lessons.

8. If Cassie ________________ (groom) the horses, George ________________ let her ride them.

Exercise 2

What would you do if things were different? Write ten unreal conditionals and read them to the class.

1. ____
2. ____
3. ____
4. ____
5. ____
6. ____
7. ____
8. ____
9. ____
10. ____

Infinitives and Gerunds

Exercise 1

*Some verbs take infinitives (*to *plus a verb); other verbs take gerunds (verb plus* -ing*). Complete the following sentences with an infinitive or a gerund.*

EXAMPLE: Cassie wanted ___*to be*___ (be) a harpist.

1. Cassie was a character who still managed ______________ (spend) most of her time in never-never land.
2. Mona, Freddy, and Joanna were discussing what they'd like ______________ (be) when they grew up.
3. Freddy planned ______________ (design) clothes.
4. Cassie gave up ______________ (attempt) ______________ (fly) like Peter Pan.
5. But she did not stop ______________ (predict) that she was going to play the harp.
6. Why don't you learn ______________ (play) an instrument you could use in the school band?
7. Before catching the 3:20 train home, Mrs. Espy decided ______________ (walk) across 57th Street.
8. Miss Lawrence will try ______________ (arrange) ______________ (teach) her.
9. A strange and beautiful sound went ______________ (vibrate) through the house.
10. Mrs. Espy considered ______________ (call) George and ______________ (warn) him about Cassie.

Exercise 2

Sometimes an infinitive or a gerund can be used after the same verb. In some cases where both are possible, the meaning of the sentence may be different depending on which is used. Can you explain the difference in the meaning of the sentences in each of the following pairs?

1.a. She stopped saying that she was going to marry Mel Ferrer.
b. She stopped to say that she was going to marry Mel Ferrer.

2.a. I'm too busy figuring out how to buy the harp.
b. I'm too busy to figure out how to buy the harp.

Follow Up

Topics for Discussion

1. Do you think it is important to take music lessons? Why or why not? What kinds of activities do you think it's most important for parents to encourage their children to do?
2. In your culture, do most parents encourage their children to play a musical instrument? Are lessons expensive in your country? Explain.
3. Following a comment of Miss Lawrence's, Mrs. Espy says that in life it's important to use everything—all one's faculties. Do you agree with her? Why or why not?
4. Cassie is very different from her sisters even though they are growing up in the same family. Why is this? In the families you know, do the brothers and sisters seem similar to or different from one another?
5. Does a child who, like Cassie, pursues a special interest miss out on something important by not having much time to spend with friends? How, if at all, can a special interest be a problem for a child?

Topics for Writing

1. Do you know a child who is as unusual or difficult as Cassie? Write a paragraph describing this child and how he or she is unusual.
2. Write an essay describing an important interest you have pursued, like chess, playing an instrument, skating, skiing, soccer, or tennis. Describe the sacrifices you had to make in order to pursue your goals.
3. What qualities do you need in order to succeed in your chosen profession? Write a paragraph in which you list these qualities and explain why they are important.
4. In an essay of three or more paragraphs, describe a person who has helped someone achieve his or her dreams. Why do you think that person was so helpful?
5. Pretend you are Cassie. Write a short story explaining how you convinced your parents to get you a harp.

UNIT 10

The Awful Fate of Melpomenus Jones

—STEPHEN LEACOCK

About the Author

The following selection is another illustration of **Stephen Leacock's** *British and Canadian background. The story presents a typically British situation—a clergyman visiting a family in their country home—in a very untypical series of events. As in the other Leacock selection, some British idioms, vocabulary, and spellings are used throughout the story. For biographical information on the author, see the introductory note to "My Financial Career," page 40.*

◆ Previewing the Story

Look at the picture, the title, and the first paragraph of the story. Answer the questions, explaining each answer.

1. What is the profession of the man in the picture? How can you tell?
2. Why are there so many cups and photographs in front of him? What do you think he is doing?
3. Does he look happy? Why do you think he is or is not?

◆ Thinking about the Topic

Think about and answer the following questions.

1. Is unannounced company acceptable in your country? If so, under what circumstances?
2. Is it possible to be too polite? What kinds of problems could result from people being too polite?
3. In your experience, is it always clear to hosts and guests when a visit is over? What makes it clear? When do confusions occur?

Some people—not you nor I, because we are so awfully[1] self-possessed[2]—but some people, find great difficulty in saying good-bye when making a call* or spending[3] the evening. As the moment draws near when the visitor feels that he is fairly entitled[4] to go away he rises and says abruptly,[5] "Well, I think I . . ." Then the people say, "Oh, must you go now? Surely it's early yet!" and a pitiful struggle[6] ensues.[7]

I think the saddest case of this kind of thing that I ever knew was that of my poor friend Melpomenus Jones, a curate[8]—such a dear[9] young man, and only twenty-three! He simply couldn't get away from people. He was too modest[10] to tell a lie, and too religious to wish to appear rude.[11] Now it happened that he went to call on* some friends of his on the very first afternoon of his summer vacation. The next six weeks were entirely his own—absolutely nothing to do. He chatted[12] awhile, drank two cups of tea, then braced[13] himself for the effort and said suddenly:

"Well, I think I . . ."

But the lady of the house said, "Oh, no! Mr. Jones, can't you really stay a little longer?"

Jones was always truthful. "Oh, yes," he said, "of course, I—er—can stay."

"Then please don't go."

He stayed. He drank eleven cups of tea. Night was falling. He rose again.

"Well now," he said shyly, "I think I really . . ."

"You must go?" said the lady politely. "I thought perhaps you could have stayed to dinner. . ."

"Oh well, so I could, you know," Jones said, "if . . ."

"Then please stay, I'm sure my husband will be delighted."

"All right," he said feebly,[14] "I'll stay," and sank back into his chair, just full of tea, and miserable.

Papa came home. They had dinner. All through the meal Jones sat planning to leave at eight-thirty. All the family wondered whether Mr. Jones was stupid and sulky,[15] or only stupid.

After dinner mamma undertook to "draw him out,"* and showed him photographs. She showed him all the family museum, several gross[16] of them—photos of papa's uncle and his wife, and mamma's brother and his little boy, an awfully interesting photo of papa's uncle's friend in his

[1] very
[2] calm, confident
[3] passing (a period of time)
[4] has a right to
[5] suddenly
[6] fight, violent effort
[7] follows
[8] clergyman
[9] well thought of
[10] shy, humble
[11] impolite, not friendly
[12] talked about unimportant things
[13] prepared
[14] weakly
[15] silently angry
[16] twelve dozen; a large amount

Bengal[17] uniform, an awfully well-taken photo of papa's grandfather's partner's dog, and an awfully wicked one of papa as the devil for a fancy-dress ball.*

At eight-thirty Jones had examined seventy-one photographs. There were about sixty-nine more that he hadn't. Jones rose.

"I must say good night now," he pleaded.[18]

"Say good night!" they said, "why it's only half-past eight! Have you anything to do?"

"Nothing," he admitted, and muttered[19] something about staying six weeks, and then laughed miserably.

Just then it turned out that the favourite child of the family, such a dear little romp,[20] had hidden Mr. Jones's hat; so papa said that he must stay, and invited him to a pipe and a chat. Papa had the pipe and gave Jones the chat, and still he stayed. Every moment he meant to take the plunge,* but couldn't. Then papa began to get very tired of Jones, and fidgeted[21] and finally said, with jocular[22] irony, that Jones had better stay all night, they could give him a shake-down.[23] Jones mistook his meaning and thanked him with tears in his eyes, and papa put Jones to bed in the spare room and cursed him heartily.[24]

After breakfast next day, papa went off to his work in the City, and left Jones playing with the baby, broken-hearted.[25] His nerve was utterly[26] gone. He was meaning to leave all day, but the thing had got on his mind and he simply couldn't. When papa came home in the evening he was surprised and chagrined[27] to find Jones still there. He thought to jockey[28] him out with a jest, and said he thought he'd have to charge him for his board,[29] he! he! The unhappy young man stared wildly for a moment, then wrung[30] papa's hand, paid him a month's board in advance, and broke down and sobbed like a child.

In the days that followed he was moody and unapproachable.[31] He lived, of course, entirely in the drawing-room,[32] and the lack of air and exercise began to tell[33] sadly on his health. He passed his time* in drinking tea and looking at the photographs. He would stand for hours gazing[34] at the photographs of papa's uncle's friend in his Bengal uniform—talking to it, sometimes swearing bitterly at it. His mind was visibly[35] failing.

At length* the crash came. They carried him upstairs in a raging delirium[36] of fever. The illness that followed was terrible. He recognised no one, not even papa's uncle's friend in his Bengal uniform. At times he

[17] large region in India
[18] begged
[19] said in a low voice not meant to be heard
[20] playful, jumping child
[21] moved restlessly
[22] humorous
[23] a bed on the floor
[24] sincerely
[25] suffering from deep sorrow
[26] completely
[27] annoyed, disappointed
[28] direct by cleverness
[29] meals by the week or month
[30] shook vigorously
[31] not friendly
[32] room in which guests are received
[33] affect
[34] looking long and steadily
[35] clearly
[36] disorienting mental disturbance

would start up from his bed and shriek, "Well, I think I . . . " and then fall back upon the pillow with a horrible laugh. Then, again, he would leap up and cry, "Another cup of tea and more photographs! More photographs! Har! Har!"

At length, after a month of agony,[37] on the last day of his vacation, he passed away.* They say that when the last moment came, he sat up in bed with a beautiful smile of confidence playing upon his face, and said, "Well—the angels are calling me; I'm afraid I really must go now. Good afternoon."

[37] great pain or suffering

And the rushing of his spirit from its prison-house was as rapid[38] as a hunted cat passing over a garden fence. ◆

[38] quick, speedy

Idioms and Phrases*

make a call	*pay a visit*
call on	*visit*
draw him out	*make him talk*
fancy-dress ball	*party at which fantastic or unusual clothing is worn*
take the plunge	*do something decisively*
passed his time	*spent his time*
at length	*finally*
passed away	*died*

Post-Reading

Comprehension

1. What was Jones's main problem? Why did he have this problem?
2. How long was his vacation supposed to last?
3. Where did he go at the start of his vacation? How long did he intend to stay there?
4. How did Jones's piety (religiousness) contribute to his problem?
5. If Jones had not been on vacation, would he have found himself in the same predicament? Why or why not?
6. What attempts did Jones make to leave? What happened?
7. How long did Jones stay with his hosts?
8. How did Jones finally leave his hosts' house?

Responding to the Story

1. What makes this story humorous?
2. What are your feelings toward Jones as you read the story?
3. Who was more responsible for Jones's long visit—Jones or his hosts? How could the problem have been resolved?
4. The comic tragedy of Melpomenus Jones is set in motion when Mamma says, "Mr. Jones, can't you stay a little longer?" How does she intend this question with *can't*? How does Mr. Jones take it?
5. Have you ever had problems leaving when you've been a visitor? Have you ever had visitors who had problems leaving? What happened?

VOCABULARY

Vocabulary Builder

Circle the letter of the correct definition for each underlined word.

1. Melpomenus Jones was never able to make a <u>rapid</u> exit.
   a. fearful c. speedy
   b. joyful d. unusual

2. The host greeted him <u>heartily</u> and offered him some tea.
   a. cautiously c. sincerely
   b. coldly d. gently

3. Mr. Jones <u>fidgeted</u> in his chair, longing to leave the house.
   a. cried c. moved restlessly
   b. played d. ate

4. Papa <u>muttered</u> under his breath as he brought out his pipe.
   a. whistled c. chuckled
   b. spoke in a low voice d. cried

5. She would not have been <u>awfully</u> upset about his leaving.
   a. very c. weakly
   b. slightly d. clearly

6. The guest and his hosts <u>chatted</u> for a while.
   a. ate snacks c. discussed important matters
   b. spoke about small things d. stayed on at the dinner table

7. "No matter what <u>ensues</u>," mamma said to herself, "I will not tell him to leave."
   a. is said c. begins
   b. is thought d. results

8. He was <u>chagrined</u> to find that his guest was there.
   a. annoyed c. unprepared
   b. confused d. delighted

9. "I must say goodnight now," he <u>pleaded</u>.
   a. called c. begged
   b. yelled d. promised

10. His hostess felt that Melpomenus Jones <u>was entitled to</u> a cup of tea.
    a. had a right to c. should not have
    b. wanted d. needed

11. Melpomenus, although very ill, lifted his head <u>feebly</u> from the pillow and began to speak.
    a. eagerly c. in pain
    b. weakly d. longingly

12. Without a <u>struggle</u>, he agreed to look through the family albums.
    a. fight c. need to do something
    b. plan d. desire

13. Melpomenus was known as a <u>modest</u> man.
    a. religious c. humble
    b. shy d. proud

14. The family was soon <u>utterly</u> annoyed at Melpomenus.
    a. completely c. amazingly
    b. quietly d. increasingly

15. When he couldn't leave, he became <u>sulky</u>.
    a. distressed c. slightly ill
    b. reckless d. silently angry

Idiom Exercise

Exercise 1: Expressions with *Mean*

a. mean = to have in mind, intend
Melpomenus Jones *meant* to stay only for tea.

b. mean business = to really mean it, be serious
Papa said he would charge Mr. Jones for his board, and he *meant business.*

c. by all means = certainly, without fail
He felt that he should, *by all means,* leave the house soon.

d. by means of = by the use of, with the help of
Papa went to work *by means of* a railroad.

Write four sentences of your own, using each of these expressions with mean.

1. ______________________________
2. ______________________________
3. ______________________________
4. ______________________________

Exercise 2: Expressions with *Draw*

a. draw up = to put in writing, compose
Melpomenus Jones *drew up* an agreement to rent a room.

b. draw out = to take out, remove; to make someone talk
He *drew* the cork *out* of the bottle.
After dinner, Mamma tried to *draw* him *out.*

c. draw a long breath = to breathe deeply when getting ready to speak or act
Melpomenus Jones *drew a long breath* when he thought he could leave.

d. draw the line = to refuse to go as far as
Although they liked him, they *drew the line* at letting him stay more than a month.

e. draw back = to move back, step backward
The children *drew back* from Melpomenus Jones after he became suddenly delirious.

Write five sentences of your own, using each of these expressions with draw.

1. ______________________________
2. ______________________________
3. ______________________________
4. ______________________________
5. ______________________________

STRUCTURE

Possessives

Rewrite the following phrases using either **'s** *or* **'** *to show possession.*

EXAMPLE: the visit of the friends
the friends' visit

1. the hat of Mr. Jones
2. the death of Melpomenus
3. board for one month

4. board for two months
5. the children of the family
6. the bedroom of the children
7. the call of the angels

Modals

Modal auxiliaries are helping verbs that are used to express intention, obligation, ability, permission, necessity, and so on.

Exercise 1

Complete the sentences below, using the modal that correctly expresses the intended meaning in the first set of parentheses.

EXAMPLE: (be necessary) Mr. Jones ___*had to*___ (had to/could) take a vacation even if he didn't want to.

1. (be able) Jones was ready to leave, but the lady of the house said, "Mr. Jones, ____________ (can't/shouldn't) you stay longer?"
2. (be able) Jones answered truthfully, "Of course, I ____________ (can/should) stay."
3. (be necessary) When night fell, Jones stood up to say that he ____________ (must/could) go.
4. (be unnecessary) Out of politeness, the lady told him that he ____________ (need not/must not) go.
5. (be strongly advised) At this point, Jones felt that he really ____________ (should/must) go.
6. (be unable) But he had his usual problem: He found that he ____________ (couldn't/can't) express this need to go.
7. (be unnecessary) When papa told him that he ____________ (needn't/mustn't) go that night, he stayed on.
8. (be possible) Papa thought that Mr. Jones ____________ (should/might) be gone when he got home from work.
9. (be able) But it was only when he heard the angels calling him that Mr. Jones ____________ (could/might) finally say goodbye.

Exercise 2

Role Play: With a few classmates, act out a situation in which you want to leave a party and your hosts are trying to convince you to stay longer. Be sure to use modals (e.g., *can/can't, must/mustn't, have to, had better, need to/needn't, should/shouldn't, could/couldn't, might*).

Past Continuous Tense

The **past continuous tense** is formed with *was/were* plus the verb + *-ing*. It describes an action that was in progress at a specific point of time in the past or at the time of another past action. Note that when one action in the past is *interrupted* by another action in the past, the action that was in progress is in the past continuous, and the action that interrupts it is in the simple past tense.

Exercise 1

Fill in the blanks with the past continuous or past tense form of the verbs indicated.

Example: He ___*was looking*___ (look) at photographs when papa ___*walked*___ (walk) in.

1. He ________ (drink) his second cup of tea when he ________ (think) about leaving.
2. Day ________ (end), and night ________ (fall) when Melpomenus ________ (look) out of the window.
3. Papa ________ (come) home, and the family then ________ (sit) down to dinner.
4. At 8:30, Jones still ________ (look) at photographs.
5. When papa ________ (leave) for work the next morning, Jones ________ (play) with the baby.
6. Jones ________ (mean) to leave all day long.
7. When papa came home in the evening, Jones ________ (be) still there.

8. Whenever people ____________________ (walk) into the drawing-room, they saw that Jones ____________________ (look) at the photographs.
9. On the last day of his vacation, Jones ____________________ (die).
10. He ____________________ (say) that he must go because the angels ____________________ (call) him.

Exercise 2

What else happened on the first evening of that fateful visit? Use your own ideas to tell what else was happening at the time of each of the following events. Complete the sentences with clauses that have a verb in the past continuous.

1. When Melpomenus arrived, mamma ____________________.
2. When Melpomenus arrived, the children ____________________.
3. While Melpomenus drank eleven cups of tea, mamma ____________________.
4. While Melpomenus drank eleven cups of tea, the children ____________________.
5. When papa walked in the door that night, Melpomenus ____________________.
6. All through their first dinner with Melpomenus, mamma and papa ____________________.
7. While Melpomenus looked at the family photos, he ____________________.
8. While papa and Melpomenus chatted, the children ____________________.
9. While papa and Melpomenus chatted, mamma ____________________.
10. When Melpomenus was shown to the spare room, the children ____________________.

Follow Up

Topics for Discussion

1. Why do you think some people stay too long?
2. What other situations can you think of in which people are polite and don't really mean what they say?
3. Mr. Jones's problems resulted in large part from his inability to take action. Have you ever found yourself in a situation where you knew you should take action but couldn't? What was the situation? Why couldn't you take action? What happened as a result?
4. Mr. Jones is unable to use a "social lie." He doesn't leave until he has a real excuse—the angels are calling him. To what extent are social lies useful? When can they cause problems?

Topics for Writing

1. In an essay of three or more paragraphs, describe a situation in which being polite got you into the same kind of trouble as it got Melpomenus Jones.
2. In 1579, John Lily said, "Fish and guests in three days are stale." In a paragraph, explain why you agree or disagree with this statement.
3. Write a short story about an interesting guest you have had. What made his or her visit interesting or memorable?
4. Write a letter to a relative inviting him or her for a visit. Be sure to specify how long you expect the relative to stay.

Unit 11

The Soft Sell

—Art Buchwald

About the Author

Art Buchwald *(1925–), a native New Yorker, first became known when he was a Paris-based columnist for the* New York Herald-Tribune. *After leaving Paris, he settled in Washington, D.C., and started writing satirically humorous articles about American politics. His syndicated column appears in over four hundred newspapers, and he is noted for his commentaries on politics and contemporary customs. In the selection below, from* I Never Danced at the White House *(1973), Buchwald makes fun of a student who thinks she is an expert on human behavior because she has studied psychology. The story tells how she tries to use her newfound knowledge on the customers who come into a store.*

◆ Previewing the Story

Look at the picture, the title, and the first paragraph of the story. Answer the questions, explaining each answer.

1. Where do you think this story takes place?
2. What is the relationship between these two women?
3. What do you think they are discussing?

◆ Thinking about the Topic

Think about and answer the following questions.

1. Whom do you ask for advice when you are trying to decide what clothing to buy?
2. How important is the salesperson's opinion to you?
3. In your country, do salespeople usually offer advice? Do they try hard to convince you to buy things?

One of the problems with today's economy is that it's very hard to find young people who are good salesmen. Many students coming out of college are more interested in a customer's motivation[1] than they are in closing[2] a sale. They also have a tendency to be too honest, which can play havoc* in the retail business.*

A friend of mine has a dress shop here in Georgetown, and she told me of the problems she had with a young lady, a psychology major,* whom she hired as a salesgirl.

This, in essence,* is what happened:

The first day a lady came in the store, and the salesgirl (let us call her Miss Brampton) asked if she could be of help.

"I'd like a suit for the fall," the lady said.

"What price range?"* Miss Brampton asked.

"It doesn't make any difference,"* the lady replied.

"Well, let me ask you this question: Do you want the suit because you need it? Or have you just had a fight with your husband and are trying to get even* by making a very expensive purchase?"[3]

"I beg your pardon?" the lady said.

"Perhaps you suspect[4] him of some infidelity,[5] and you think this is the only way you can get back* at him."

"I have no idea what you're talking about," the customer said.

"Spending money in anger is a very expensive form of hostility.[6] My advice to you is to think it over for a few days. Try to patch up* your differences. Buying a new suit won't save your marriage."

"Thank you very much," the customer said frostily[7] and left the store.

"She's angry with me now," Miss Brampton told the dress shop owner, "but in a week she'll be grateful I talked her out of it."*

My friend the shop proprietor[8] decided to let the incident[9] pass; but that afternoon another customer came in, and Miss Brampton asked if she could be of help.

The lady said, "I need something really exciting. I'm going to the Kennedy Center, and I want a dress that will knock everyone dead."*

Miss Brampton said, "We have some lovely evening dresses over here for insecure[10] people."

"Insecure people?"

[1] reason for doing something

[2] completing

[3] something bought

[4] have an idea or feeling

[5] disloyalty or unfaithfulness

[6] undirected anger

[7] coldly; in an unfriendly way

[8] owner

[9] happening

[10] unsure, without self-confidence

"Oh, yes. Didn't you know that clothes are one of the main ways women compensate[11] for insecurity?"

"I'm not insecure," the lady said angrily.

"Then why do you want to knock them dead at the Kennedy Center? Why can't you be accepted for yourself instead of what you wear? You are a very attractive person, and you have an inner beauty you try to disguise.[12] I can sell you a new dress that will attract attention,* but then you would never know if it were you or the dress that made people stop and stare."[13]

By this time the dress shop owner decided to step in.

"Miss Brampton, if the lady wants an evening dress, let her see our evening dresses."

"No," the customer said. "Your girl is right. Why spend five hundred dollars to get a few compliments from people who really don't care what I wear? Thank you for helping me, young lady. It's true I've been insecure all these years and didn't even know it."

The customer walked out of the store.

The final straw* for the dress store owner took place an hour later when a coed[14] came in to buy a hotpants[15] outfit, and Miss Brampton gave her thirty minutes[16] on women's lib[17] and then said, "All you do when you buy hotpants is become a sex object."

That night the dress shop owner put a sign in the window: HELP WANTED—NO PSYCHOLOGY MAJORS NEED APPLY. ◆

[11] make up
[12] hide
[13] look fixedly
[14] female student at a coeducational university
[15] very short shorts
[16] thirty-minute speech
[17] liberation

Idioms and Phrases*

soft sell	*a manner of selling without pressuring the customer*
play havoc	*cause ruin and chaos*
retail business	*stores that sell goods to the public*
psychology major	*student who specializes in the study of psychology in college*
in essence	*basically*
what price range?	*how much money do you want to spend?*
it doesn't make any difference	*it's not important, it doesn't matter*
get even	*get revenge*
get back at him	*hurt (him) back*
patch up	*put together in a hurried way; repair the damage*

talked her out of it	*persuaded her to change her mind*
knock everyone dead	*impress everyone*
attract attention	*get the attention of others*
final straw	*the event or happening that made it intolerable*

Post-Reading

Comprehension

Based on the story, is the statement true or false? If it's false, explain why.

1. It's easy to find good salespeople.
2. Honesty is the best policy in the retail business.
3. According to Miss Brampton, the woman who wanted a suit was insecure.
4. The woman who wanted a suit appreciated Miss Brampton's advice.
5. The woman who came in to buy an evening gown appreciated Miss Brampton's advice.
6. Miss Brampton told the coed not to buy hotpants.
7. According to Miss Brampton, a woman who buys hotpants becomes a sex object.
8. The store proprietor fired Miss Brampton.
9. The proprietor will hire only psychology majors from now on.

Responding to the Story

1. What do you think motivated Miss Brampton to act the way she did?
2. How could the store owner have prevented Miss Brampton from losing the sales?
3. What job might be more suitable for Miss Brampton?
4. What field of study do you feel prepares someone to be a good salesperson? Why?
5. How would you have reacted to Miss Brampton's remarks if you were the lady who wanted the suit? the lady who wanted an evening dress? the coed who wanted hotpants?
6. What do you think would have happened had Miss Brampton not been fired? Would she finally have made some sales? Or would the shop have gone out of business?

Vocabulary

Vocabulary Builder

Answer the questions yes or no and briefly explain your answers.

1. Is it polite to *stare*?
2. Are *insecure* people more nervous than other people?
3. Is *infidelity* a major cause of divorce?
4. Do you ever try to *disguise* your *hostility*?
5. Do you *suspect* the author is not really serious?
6. When someone looks at you *frostily*, are you upset?
7. Do you agree with the way the *proprietor* of the dress shop handled the hotpants incident?

Idiom Exercise

Answer the questions.

1. How did Miss Brampton's psychology *play havoc* with the retail business?
2. When you try to *get back* at someone, do you sometimes hurt yourself?
3. What do you wear when you try to *knock everyone dead*?
4. Do you think that the saleswoman tried to *patch up* her differences with the proprietor?
5. What was the *final straw* in the relationship between Miss Brampton and the proprietor?

Clothing

1. Suppose you were going on (a) a business trip to Alaska and (b) a vacation trip to Florida. Make a list of the clothing you would need in each place and the fabrics best suited for each climate.
2. If you had to have your clothes altered, would you know what instructions to give the tailor or dressmaker? On the next page are sketches of a dress, a pair of slacks, and a jacket. Pretend that they are (a) too large and (b) too small for you, and write instructions for the necessary alterations. Be specific about what you want done, and give specific measurements.

Example: Take up the hem by three-quarters of an inch. Take in the waist by one inch. . . .

belt
belt loop
pleat
zipper
SLACKS
crease
cuff
shoe
JACKET
collar
shirt
lapel
button
necktie
sleeve
button
pocket
buttonhole
collar
neckline
pocket
belt
belt buckle
waistline
button
DRESS
skirt
pleat
hemline
leg

Advise and Advice

***Advise** is a verb, while **advice** is a noun. Supply the correct word in the following sentences. Put verbs in the correct form.*

EXAMPLE: My ____*advice*____ to you is to think it over for a few days.

1. The shop proprietor __________ Miss Brampton to find another job.
2. I would __________ you to buy the blue suit.
3. That was sound __________.
4. When I want your __________, I'll ask for it.
5. Please __________ me on what to wear to the Kennedy Center.
6. Giving __________ is easy; following it is difficult.
7. Don't give __________ where it's not wanted.
8. The saleswoman __________ her to buy the blue dress because it suited her.
9. My __________ is to buy a suit for the fall.
10. A marriage counselor—and not a salesperson—__________ people about patching up their differences.

STRUCTURE

Infinitives and Gerunds

Complete the following sentences with an infinitive or a gerund from the base verb given in parentheses.

EXAMPLES: Jane avoided ____*thinking*____ it over.
(think)

My advice to you is ____*to think*____ it over for a few days.
(think)

1. These days, it is very unusual __________ young people
(find)
who are good salespersons.

2. Have you ever considered __________ a hotpants outfit?
(buy)

3. She couldn't resist ____________________ that dress.
   (try on)
4. Why do you want ____________________ them dead?
   (knock)
5. The saleswoman promised ____________________ customers.
   (encourage)
6. The woman expected ____________________ a lovely evening
   (purchase)
   gown.
7. The proprietor hoped the saleswoman would keep on
   ____________________. She didn't want ____________________ money.
   (sell) (lose)
8. Miss Brampton was more interested in a customer's motivation than in
   ____________________ a sale.
   (close)
9. The dress shop failed ____________________ money while Miss
   (make)
   Brampton was employed there.
10. The proprietor delayed ____________________ Miss Brampton as long
    (fire)
    as possible.
11. Miss Brampton claims ____________________ an expert on human
    (be)
    behavior.
12. The final straw came when she decided ____________________ the
    (discourage)
    sale of a pair of hotpants.
13. The customer needed ____________________ a new suit.
    (get)
14. The owner didn't want ____________________ ____________________
    (risk) (insult)
    the customers.
15. Why did you refuse ____________________ her the dress?
    (sell)
16. "Have you considered ____________________ another job?" the
    (take)
    proprietor asked.

Relative Clauses

*Combine the two sentences by making the second sentence a relative clause. Be sure to use a correct relative pronoun (*who, that, which, *or* whose*) where a relative pronoun is needed and to include commas where needed. If a relative pronoun is optional, do* not *include it. Omit unnecessary words.*

EXAMPLES: I want a new dress. I want it to knock them dead.
I want a new dress that will knock them dead.

There's no point spending money so that people will pay you compliments. You don't need those compliments.
There's no point spending money so that people will pay you compliments you don't need.

1. Many young people have a tendency to be too honest. This tendency to be too honest can play havoc in the retail business.
2. These are just expensive clothes. Women use expensive clothes to compensate for feeling insecure.
3. You have an inner beauty. You try to disguise this inner beauty.
4. She is buying that suit to get back at her husband. She suspects her husband of infidelity.
5. The second customer didn't need an evening dress. Her motive was insecurity.
6. Miss Brampton discouraged customers from making purchases. This is why the store owner fired her.
7. Miss Brampton is not effective as a saleswoman. Miss Brampton is a psychology major.
8. The shop owner in the story has had trouble with saleswomen. Her dress shop is in Georgetown.

Sentence Builder: Constructions with *It*

In certain constructions, it *does not have a meaning or refer to anything but simply fills the subject position in the sentence. Following the patterns shown, change the sentences to sentences with* it.

A. PATTERN: Young people who are good salespeople are hard to find. —>
It is hard to find young people who are good salespeople.

1. Hotpants that fit well are hard to find.
2. Expensive evening dresses are easy to find.
3. Insecurities can be hard to compensate for.

B. PATTERN: That I've been insecure is true. —>
It is true that I've been insecure.

4. That Miss Brampton would be fired was inevitable.
5. That Miss Brampton was not an effective salesperson was clear.
6. That the customer was displeased was obvious to everyone but Miss Brampton.

What Clauses for Emphasis

The use of a *what* clause at the beginning of a sentence can make the statement more emphatic. For example, *When you wear hotpants you become a sex object* can be stated more emphatically as *What you do when you wear hotpants is become a sex object.* In addition to *what,* the appropriate form of *be* is added to the sentence, following the *what* clause. This construction is used mainly in spoken English.

Change the following sentences to constructions with what *clauses, following the pattern in the example.*

EXAMPLE: She wanted a suit for the fall.
What she wanted was a suit for the fall.

1. She suspected him of some infidelity.
2. She wanted to get even.
3. I would advise you to think it over for a few days.
4. The customer felt considerable anger.
5. The lady wanted something really exciting.
6. She wanted to go to the Kennedy Center and impress everyone.
7. People really care about your inner beauty.
8. The shop owner now wants a business major.

Role Play: With a partner, act out the roles of salesperson and shopper. Choose one of the following possibilities to act out. Use some constructions with *what* clauses for emphasis.

1. Miss Brampton is hired at another store of some other kind—not a dress shop—and uses the same approach there.
2. A business major has been hired at the dress shop and uses a hard sell (i.e., a high-pressure) approach.

Follow Up

Topics for Discussion

1. Before you make a purchase in a store, do you think it over carefully, or do you buy on impulse? What was your last clothing purchase, and why did you decide to buy that particular item?
2. If you were the owner of a dress shop, would you hire psychology majors? Can you name any instances where using psychology might help you to close a sale?

3. Suppose the main character in this story were a male psychology major who was working in a store that sold men's clothing. What would he stress in order to sell a suit? a sweater? a pair of jeans? Why?
4. Teenagers often buy their own clothes. If you were trying to sell to someone between fifteen and eighteen years old, what kinds of things would you stress?
5. When choosing a place to buy clothes, what do you look for—low prices, interested and knowledgeable salespeople, latest styles, or something else?
6. The soft-sell approach, of which Miss Brampton provides an extreme example, involves not pressuring customers. The hard-sell approach, in contrast, involves high pressure. Which approach do you prefer as a customer? Which do you think is more effective?

Topics for Writing

1. In several paragraphs, describe an item of clothing you have recently purchased. Write about its style and color, as well as about how you feel when you wear it.
2. Many people go shopping when they feel depressed and want to cheer themselves up. Have you ever done this? If so, write a short anecdote that describes one of those shopping trips. Did you feel better afterwards? How long did that feeling last?
3. In groups of three, write an advertisement in which you try to sell a large-screen television. Make sure that you mention all the features it has, how much it costs, and the methods of payment. Make sure to use an approach that will motivate people to want to buy the TV.
4. Write a list of do's and don'ts for shopping. For example: compare prices, don't buy on impulse. Then write an essay of several paragraphs, in which you mention and briefly discuss these do's and don'ts.
5. You've invited a friend to meet your parents, and you don't like what she/he is planning to wear. Write a dialogue in which you try to convince her/him to wear something else without hurting her/his feelings.
6. Might Miss Brampton have changed a customer's life? Write a short story about one of the three women who came into the store. Assume that she kept thinking about what Miss Brampton said and that, as a result, the next time her husband, boyfriend, or friends saw her, they noticed great changes. What were these changes? What happened next?

UNIT 12

Glove Purchase in Gibraltar

—SAMUEL CLEMENS
(MARK TWAIN)

ABOUT THE AUTHOR

SAMUEL CLEMENS *(1835–1910) was born in Missouri, grew up near the Mississippi River, and left school at the age of twelve when his father died. He then held a variety of odd jobs, mainly as a printer and as apprentice to the pilot of a steamboat on the Mississippi, the greatest river in the United States. He adopted the pen name Mark Twain, which was a common phrase used by river pilots. He is considered the best—and the most widely read—American writer of humor and satire. His books include the travel books* Roughing It *(1872) and* Life on the Mississippi *(1883) and the world-renowned classics,* The Adventures of Tom Sawyer *(1876) and* Huckleberry Finn *(1884).*

In June of 1867, Twain joined a group that was traveling on the ship Quaker City *to the Mediterranean and Palestine. The book that grew out of his journey,* The Innocents Abroad *(1869), established his literary reputation. The ship stopped in Gibraltar, and the following selection describes one of Twain's experiences there.*

◆ PREVIEWING THE STORY

Look at the picture, the title, and the first paragraph of the story. Answer the questions explaining each answer.

1. Where are the man and woman? What are they doing?
2. What is wrong with the glove on the man's hand? Is it new or old? What is happening in the picture?

◆ THINKING ABOUT THE TOPIC

1. What are some sales techniques you've seen used by salespeople, in the United States or in your country?
2. Do you think that people might shop differently when they are visiting a place than they would if they lived there? If so, how?
3. Gibraltar may be known for its leather products. What products is your country known for?

Every now and then my glove purchase in Gibraltar last night intrudes[1] itself upon me. Dan and the ship's surgeon and I had been up to the great square, listening to the music of the fine military bands, and contemplating[2] English and Spanish female loveliness and fashion, and, at nine o'clock, were on our way to the theatre, when we met the General, the Judge, the Commodore, the Colonel, and the Commissioner of the United States of America to Europe, Asia, and Africa, who had been to the Club House, to register their several titles and impoverish[3] the bill of fare,* and they told us to go over to the little variety store, near the Hall of Justice, and buy some kid[4] gloves. They said they were elegant, and very moderate[5] in price. It seemed a stylish thing to go to the theatre in kid gloves, and we acted upon the hint.[6] A very handsome young lady in the store offered me a pair of blue gloves. I did not want blue, but she said they would look very pretty on a hand like mine. The remark touched[7] me tenderly. I glanced furtively[8] at my hand, and somehow it did seem rather a comely[9] member.[10] I tried a glove on my left, and blushed a little. Manifestly[11] the size was too small for me. But I felt gratified[12] when she said:

"Oh, it is just right!"—yet I knew it was no such thing.

I tugged[13] at it diligently,[14] but it was discouraging work. She said:

"Ah! I see *you* are accustomed to* wearing kid gloves—but some gentlemen are *so* awkward[15] about putting them on."

It was the last compliment I had expected. I only understand putting on the buckskin[16] article perfectly. I made another effort, and tore the glove from the base[17] of the thumb into the palm of the hand—and tried to hide the rent.[18] She kept up her compliments, and I kept up my determination to deserve them or die:

"Ah, you have had experience!" (A rip down the back of the hand.) "They are just right for you—your hand is very small—if they tear you need not pay for them." (A rent across the middle.) "I can always tell when a gentleman understands putting on kid gloves. There is a grace about it that only comes with long practice." (The whole afterguard of the glove "fetched away,"[19] as the sailors say, the fabric parted[20] across the knuckles,° and nothing was left but a melancholy[21] ruin.)[22]

[1] forces

[2] looking at; thinking about

[3] cause to become poor or less

[4] leather from a young goat's skin

[5] inexpensive

[6] suggestion

[7] affected

[8] secretly

[9] nice-looking (old use)

[10] part of the body

[11] obviously

[12] pleased

[13] pulled

[14] with great care

[15] clumsy

[16] a type of leather

[17] bottom

[18] tear

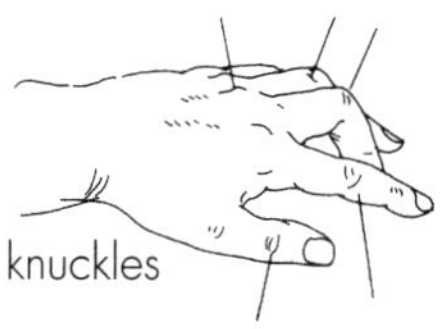

[19] came apart

[20] separated

[21] sad

[22] damaged remains

I was too much flattered[23] to make an exposure, and throw the merchandise[24] on the angel's hands. I was hot, vexed,[25] confused, but still happy; but I hated the other boys for taking such an absorbing[26] interest in the proceedings.[27] I wished they were in Jericho. I felt exquisitely mean[28] when I said cheerfully,—

[23] pleased by a compliment
[24] item(s) for sale
[25] annoyed
[26] completely taking up the attention or thoughts
[27] actions
[28] ungenerous

"This one does very well; it fits elegantly. I like a glove that fits. No, never mind,* ma'am, never mind; I'll put the other on in the street. It is warm here."

It *was* warm. It was the warmest place I ever was in. I paid the bill, and as I passed out with a fascinating bow, I thought I detected[29] a light in the woman's eye that was gently ironical; and when I looked back from the street, and she was laughing all to herself about something or other, I said to myself, with withering[30] sarcasm, "Oh, certainly; *you* know how to put on kid gloves, don't you?—a self-complacent[31] ass,[32] ready to be flattered out of your senses by every petticoat[33] that chooses to take the trouble to do it!"

[29] saw
[30] causing somebody to feel ashamed or confused
[31] satisfied with oneself
[32] idiot; donkey
[33] woman's underskirt (slang: woman) (not current)

The silence of the boys annoyed me. Finally, Dan said, musingly:[34]

[34] thoughtfully, in a dreamy way

"Some gentlemen don't know how to put on kid gloves at all; but some do."

And the doctor said (to the moon, I thought):

"But it is always easy to tell when a gentleman is used to putting on kid gloves."

Dan soliloquized,[35] after a pause:

"Ah, yes; there is a grace[36] about it that only comes with long, very long practice."

[35] talked to himself
[36] elegant style

"Yes, indeed, I've noticed that when a man hauls[37] on a kid glove like he was dragging[38] a cat out of an ash-hole by the tail, *he* understands putting on kid gloves; *he's* had ex—"

[37] pulls with effort
[38] pulling

"Boys, enough of a thing's enough! You think you are very smart, I suppose, but I don't. And if you go and tell any of those old gossips[39] in the ship about this thing, I'll never forgive you for it; that's all."

[39] people who talk about others

They let me alone* then, for the time being. We always let each other alone in time to prevent ill[40] feeling from spoiling a joke. But they had bought gloves, too, as I did. We threw all the purchases away together this morning. They were coarse,[41] unsubstantial,[42] freckled[43] all over with broad yellow splotches,[44] and could neither stand wear nor public exhibition. We had entertained an angel unawares, but we did not take her in.* She did that for us. ◆

[40] bad
[41] of poor quality, rough
[42] weak, thin
[43] dotted
[44] spots

Idioms and Phrases*

bill of fare	*menu*
be accustomed to	*be in the habit of*
never mind	*don't trouble about it*
let me alone	*stayed away from me; didn't bother me*
did not take her in	*did not fool her; did not provide hospitality*

Post-Reading

Comprehension

1. At the beginning of the story, where was the narrator and who was with him?
2. Who suggested to the narrator and his companions that they buy gloves? What kind of gloves did they intend to buy and where did they intend to wear them?
3. Describe the gloves that the narrator tried on. How well did they fit him?
4. What sales methods did the saleswoman use in order to get him to buy the gloves?
5. Why did the narrator's friends tease him so much?
6. What did they all do with the gloves they had purchased?

Responding to the Story

1. How does this selection reflect the title of the book from which it was taken (*The Innocents Abroad*)?
2. Do you think the glove purchase would have occurred if the saleswoman hadn't used flattery? if the salesperson had used flattery, but had been a man? if the narrator had been in his hometown? Explain your answers.
3. How does the narrator seem to feel about the experience and his behavior when it's all over?
4. What characteristics of human nature does this story illustrate (through the narrator and the other characters)? Do you agree that this is how people are? Why or why not?
5. Has a salesperson ever talked you into buying something you didn't want to buy? How did this happen? Did the salesperson use flattery?

VOCABULARY

Vocabulary Builder

Circle the letter of the correct definition for each underlined word.

1. A coarse fabric is

   a. soft c. rough
   b. spotted d. stylish

2. In being embarrassed by the proceedings, the narrator was embarrassed by the

   a. prices c. purchase
   b. flattery d. actions

3. An awkward motion is

   a. clumsy c. funny
   b. graceful d. magnificent

4. A person who is impoverished is

   a. poor c. important
   b. rich d. unknown

5. A person who is gratified by someone's comments is

   a. pleased c. surprised
   b. upset d. irritated

6. Absorbing proceedings are

   a. long c. interesting
   b. dull d. quick

7. Contemplating a purchase is

   a. describing it c. thinking about it
   b. regretting it d. making it

8. A person who intrudes upon another

   a. forces himself on the other c. takes something from the other
   b. talks about the other d. makes a joke about the other

9. When the narrator tugged at the glove, he

   a. pulled it c. removed it
   b. looked quickly at it d. tore it

10. To put a glove on furtively would be to put it on

    a. secretly c. clumsily
    b. slowly d. gracefully

11. Kid gloves are made of
    a. suede
    b. goatskin
    c. cotton
    d. wool

12. If the gloves looked like a ruin, they looked
    a. like cheap copies of something
    b. of poor quality
    c. newly made
    d. badly damaged

13. A person who is vexed at his friends is
    a. annoyed
    b. complimented
    c. pleased
    d. teased

14. Something that is manifestly untrue is
    a. obviously a lie
    b. partially a lie
    c. completely true
    d. greatly exaggerated

15. When Dan soliloquizes, he speaks
    a. to himself
    b. to a group
    c. in a whisper
    d. very loudly

16. If there are ill feelings in a group, people have feelings that are
    a. hidden
    b. lacking
    c. bad
    d. confused

Idiom Exercise: Idioms with *Hand*

Exercise 1

Read the following definitions and examples of idioms, phrases, and compound words that involve hand.

1. hand in glove = very close or friendly; working together; in very close agreement or cooperation, especially for bad purposes

   The tourist guide and the store owner sometimes work *hand in glove* to bring tourists to a store.

2. handle with kid gloves = to treat very gently and carefully

   He is so sensitive that he has to be *handled with kid gloves.*

3. hand down = to give after outgrowing or to arrange to leave after death

   Mary will have her mother's kid gloves because they are *handed down* in the family.

4. hand in hand = holding hands

   The commodore and his wife walked *hand in hand* down the street.

5. hand it to = to admit the excellence of, give credit or praise to

   You have to *hand it to* that salesperson; she always makes a sale.

(Continued on next page)

6. out of hand = out of control

   The joking about his purchase got *out of hand.*

7. hand-pick = to choose very carefully

   Because the job was difficult, the general *hand-picked* his assistant.

8. hands down = easily

   Because of the excellence of the food, the restaurant won the "best food" award *hands down.*

9. a free hand = great freedom

   The store manager gave the salesperson *a free hand* in ordering new gloves.

10. lend a hand = to help

    When his friends were in trouble, he never hesitated to *lend a hand.*

Exercise 2

Write a sentence using each of these expressions with hand.

1. ______________________________
2. ______________________________
3. ______________________________
4. ______________________________
5. ______________________________
6. ______________________________
7. ______________________________
8. ______________________________
9. ______________________________
10. ______________________________

Word Forms

Fill in the blanks with the correct form of the words listed.

1. intruded, intruding, intrusion, intruder
   a. Your opening my mail is an unnecessary ______________ on my privacy.
   b. "I hope I'm not ______________," he said as he walked into the room.
   c. The sound of the military band ______________ on our conversation.
   d. The ______________ interrupted her efforts to make a sale.

2. flattering, flatterer, flattered, flattery
   a. "____________________ will get you nowhere," she said sweetly.
   b. For her, blue is a very ____________________ color.
   c. He felt very ____________________ when the salesperson told him he had nice hands.
   d. A ____________________ is often not sincere.
3. absorb, absorbing, absorption, absorbed
   a. I hated the boys for taking such an ____________________ interest in the proceedings.
   b. They listened to the story with complete ____________________.
   c. They found it difficult to ____________________ all the details of the story.
   d. He was so ____________________ in buying gloves that he didn't hear his friends come into the store.
4. contemplated, contemplation, contemplating, contemplative
   a. Are you ____________________ a trip to Europe this summer?
   b. He isn't usually a very ____________________ person.
   c. We ____________________ buying souvenirs, but decided against it.
   d. Her ____________________ of my hand made me nervous.

STRUCTURE

Conjunctions: *And* versus *But*

Exercise 1

Complete the following compound sentences by choosing and *or* but.

EXAMPLES: The young lady offered me a pair of gloves, ____*and*____ I put them on.

Some gentlemen don't know how to put on kid gloves at all, ____*but*____ some do.

1. It seemed a stylish thing to go to the theater in kid gloves, ____________________ we acted upon the hint.
2. I did not want blue, ____________________ she said they would look very pretty on a hand like mine.
3. I tugged at it diligently, ____________________ I couldn't get it on my hand.

(Continued on next page)

4. Some gentlemen are so awkward, ________________ you are so graceful.
5. She kept up her compliments, ________________ I kept up my determination to deserve them or die.
6. The fabric parted across the knuckles, ________________ nothing was left but a melancholy ruin.
7. I was hot, vexed, and confused, ________________ I was still happy.
8. You think you are very smart, I suppose, ________________ I don't.
9. The gloves were coarse, unsubstantial, and splotched, ________________ they could neither stand wear nor public exhibition.
10. We had entertained an angel unawares, ________________ we did not take her in.

Exercise 2

Write seven compound sentences with and *and* but, *but leave blanks where these conjunctions would go. Trade papers with a partner, and fill in the blanks. Then check answers with your partner. If, for any sentences,* and *and* but *are both possible, discuss why and discuss whether there is any difference in the meaning.*

Literary Language: Similes, Metaphors, and Double Meanings

Similes and metaphors are comparisons, often unusual and unexpected comparisons, which can make an author's writing more interesting. A **simile** is a comparison that uses *like* or *as*. In the story, the doctor says, "I've noticed that when a man hauls on a kid glove like he was dragging a cat out of an ash-hole by the tail, he understands putting on kid gloves." This comparison of putting on a kid glove to dragging a cat out of an ash-can gives the reader a vivid picture and adds to the humor. Just as there is nothing elegant about dragging a cat out of a hole, there was nothing elegant about the way the doctor's friend was putting on the glove.

A **metaphor** is a comparison that does *not* use *like* or *as*. For example, the narrator says he was too flattered to "throw the merchandise on the angel's hands." He is comparing the young lady in the store to an angel. But he makes the comparison by substituting "the angel" for "the young lady," therefore not using *like* or *as*.

Exercise 1

Write three sentences that are related to the characters and events in the story and make sure that each contains a simile or a metaphor.

EXAMPLES: Simile: The glove fit his hand like the glass slipper fit Cinderella's stepsister's foot.

Metaphor: He stared at the mistake on his hand.

Exercise 2

In a group of three, write and then act out for the class a humorous dialogue in which a salesperson uses flattery and other such techniques to try to sell something that is very obviously not much good. The customer is tempted by the flattery, but is with a friend, who tries to point out the problems. Include some similes and metaphors in the dialogue. These can be exaggerated and thereby contribute to the humor.

Exercise 3

Double meanings can also be an important tool for writers, especially when they are used satirically. Think about the last two sentences of the story: "We had entertained an angel unawares, but we did not take her in. She did that for us." Using a dictionary if necessary, figure out how entertain *and* take in *both have more than one meaning. Because these words have more than one meaning, the sentences do as well. What are these meanings? How are these sentences, with their double meanings, an effective ending for this story?*

Complex Sentences

Writing can be made more effective by combining simple sentences to form complex sentences.

Combine each set of simple sentences below into a single complex sentence. Omit and add words as needed. Do not look back at the story until you have written your sentences. There are various ways to form these sentences; your sentences don't have to be the same as the sentences in the story.

EXAMPLES: The gloves were coarse.

The gloves were freckled all over with broad yellow splotches.

For these reasons they could not be worn. —>

Because the gloves were coarse and freckled all over with broad yellow splotches, they could not be worn.

1. Dan had been up to the great square.

   The ship's surgeon had been up to the great square.

   I had been up to the great square.

   On our way to the theater we met the General, the Judge, the Commodore, the Colonel, and the Commissioner.

   They told us to buy some kid gloves.

2. I paid the bill.

   At the same time I thought I detected a light in the woman's eye.

   The light was gently ironical.

   She was laughing all to herself about something or other.

Conditional: Possible

The conditional statement is composed of two clauses, the ***if* clause** and the **result clause.** One type of conditional statement is used when it is possible for the condition to be fulfilled. It is expressed by using the present tense in the *if* clause and the future tense in the *result* clause.

EXAMPLE: If I travel, I ____*will*____ go by boat.

Exercise 1

Write a result clause for each of the following conditional statements. Choose your own verbs.

1. If I walk to the park, I ____________________.
2. If you make too much noise, you ____________________.
3. If I learn to drive, I ____________________.
4. If we buy the theater tickets, we ____________________.
5. If we dine early, we ____________________.
6. If he goes on vacation, he ____________________.
7. If I get lost, I ____________________.
8. If she sells many pairs of gloves, she ____________________.
9. If it rains, it ____________________.

Exercise 2

Make up ten of your own sentences using the if *clause and* result *clause format.*

FOLLOW UP

Topics for Discussion

1. What are some other ways in which a tourist can be "taken in" in a foreign country? Has this ever happened to you?
2. Certain countries are noted for certain products, and shopping for those products is part of the pleasure of being in that country. What countries would you like to travel to in order to shop? What would you like to buy in those countries?
3. What things did you buy when you were on vacation? Why did you buy them?
4. What other kinds of things do you enjoy doing when you are visiting a foreign country?

5. Are you susceptible to flattery? If someone wants something from you, would they be able to get it by flattering you? Why or why not?
6. Are there any advantages to having an embarrassing experience happen in the company of friends? Or would it be better to be alone? Explain your answer.

Topics for Writing

1. Write a summary of the story. (Remember that a summary should include only important facts and events; do *not* include details.)
2. Write about a purchase you made when you were on vacation. Why did you buy it? When you got home, were you happy that you had bought it?
3. Write about an "Innocents Abroad" type of experience that you have had. Try to write the story in a humorous tone.
4. Write a dialogue in which the saleswoman uses the same approach as in the selection but has a customer who turns out to be much less innocent.
5. Have you ever dealt over a period of time with a salesperson that you either especially liked or especially disliked? In a three-paragraph essay, describe his or her characteristics and sales approach.

UNIT 13

What Do You Do with Your Old Coffee Grounds?

—HOWARD LINDSAY

About the Author

Howard Lindsay *(1889–1968) was a noted playwright, director, and actor. In 1934 he began a collaboration with Russel Crouse that was to last twenty-eight years. Together they wrote the play* State of the Union, *which won a Pulitzer Prize in 1946. They also wrote the movie version of* The Sound of Music *in 1959, which became one of the most financially successful motion pictures in its day. Lindsay is best known for his play* Life with Father*—based on the novel by Clarence Day—which set a Broadway record of 3,224 performances over seven years. Lindsay played the father opposite his wife, Dorothy Stickney, as the mother. She is the bride he describes in the following story. They were married in 1927.*

◆ Previewing the Story

Look at the picture, the title, and the first paragraph of the story. Answer the questions, explaining each answer.

1. What do you think the title means? How does it connect with the picture?
2. Who are the people in the picture?
3. Describe the expressions of the people in the picture.
4. Which of the characters might be asking the question in the title? Can you guess why?

◆ Thinking about the Topic

Think about and answer the following questions.

1. In your country, what is the usual way of making coffee?
2. Have you heard of any uses for old coffee grounds? If so, what?
3. Does your attitude toward spending money differ from that of your parents? If so, how does it differ from theirs?

We had been married for six months before my wife and my mother met. The first confrontation[1] had its surprises as well as its difficulties. The first surprise came to my mother. She knew I had married an actress. I am sure she had imagined her to be somewhat[2] like the lush[3] female on the poster of "The Girl from Rector's." She was not prepared for that wide-eyed chit of a child* stretched out on the couch, her pale forehead contracted[4] in pain. I explained to mother that Dorothy was not well. She had a severe[5] headache. All her life mother had been subject to* what were then called "sick headaches" and she was instantly sympathetic. What we could not tell mother was that Dorothy was suffering from her first hangover.[6]

The night before, Dorothy and I had been down in the Village at a party. It was given by one of the gayest and most charming couples in New York, Miriam Hopkins and Bill Parker. We drank more than our wont.[7] At that time Dorothy hadn't cultivated[8] any wont and knew nothing of the consequences[9] of drinking too much. We had talked and laughed and sung and at six in the morning Miriam cooked us some breakfast. There just aren't any parties like that anymore, unless they are being given by people who are as young now as we were then. That Dorothy was to meet her mother-in-law the next day seemed unimportant.

Mother was a small, delicate-looking woman, a wisp[10] of New England granite.[11] We had a part-time maid, which I knew struck mother as* an extravagance,[12] but she held her peace.* I had ordered a simple and frugal[13] dinner which mother seemed to enjoy. Dorothy sat with us at the table, ate little, and contributed less to the conversation. After the coffee had been served, mother held Dorothy's eye* and asked, "What do you do with your old coffee grounds?" The throb[14] in Dorothy's temple[15] jumped into high gear.* Had my wife been in perfect health and high spirits,* I submit[16] this was an unfair question. "I don't know what we do with them," she stammered,[17] looking very guilty. "I guess we just throw them away." "You can use them for flavoring," mother said smugly.[18] "Make your own coffee jello."

I, too, had been bewildered[19] by mother's question, but now I knew that mother had accepted our marriage and was trying to contribute to

[1] unfriendly meeting

[2] in a way

[3] large, healthy

[4] pulled together; wrinkled

[5] serious; painful

[6] unpleasant physical effects of drinking too much alcohol

[7] custom, habit

[8] developed

[9] effects, results

[10] small piece

[11] very hard stone

[12] something that cost too much; an extreme

[13] economical, inexpensive

[14] pulsing pain

[15] side of the forehead

[16] state an opinion

[17] spoke haltingly

[18] in a self-satisfied way

[19] very puzzled

it. And all she had to contribute were the economies that a lifetime of being poor had taught her. She knew all the shortcuts and shifts[20] that would save a penny, and to her not saving a penny when you could was one of the deadly sins. A worse sin, if there was one, was spending a penny you didn't need to spend.

Ten years before my marriage I had been able to bring mother to New York for a visit. I thought she deserved a fling[21] and in my ignorance thought she would enjoy one. The first night I took her to dinner at Mouquin's. In those days you could get a good Italian dinner anywhere for seventy-five cents and if you knew your New York you could get a substantial[22] meal for forty or fifty cents. Mouquin's was a French restaurant better and more expensive than the average. Mother discovered that the cheapest meal we could get there was the dollar and twenty-five cent dinner. I ordered one for each of us. She couldn't eat a morsel.[23] While the waiter served the courses and then removed her untouched plates mother sat there and silently wept.[24]

Later when mother's health was fading[25] I would bring her flowers. It was no fun for either of us. No smile of pleasure would light her face. She would shake her head in a pained way and murmur, "They'll be dead in a day or two and a whole dollar wasted." The uses of adversity[26] are not always sweet, Mr. Shakespeare; they can be horrible and scarifying.[27]

When she died, mother left over five thousand dollars she had scrimped together* somehow. She could have well spent this on herself, but not with any pleasure. I can't say I learned the value of money from my mother because I don't think she knew the value of it. But my attitude toward money does stem from* her. I have always followed the lesson she unwittingly[28] taught me: Spend It While You Have It. ◆

[20] tricks
[21] short period of fun and excitement
[22] large
[23] mouthful, small bite
[24] cried
[25] failing; disappearing slowly
[26] hard times
[27] frightening; leaving a wound
[28] unknowingly; without meaning to

IDIOMS AND PHRASES*

coffee grounds	*ground coffee beans that have been used*
chit of a child	*very young, slim looking person*
subject to	*likely to get or have*
struck mother as	*seemed to her to be*
held her peace	*kept quiet*

held Dorothy's eye	*caught her attention*
high gear	*high speed*
high spirits	*good humor, happy state*
scrimped together	*saved by not spending much*
stem from	*come from*

POST-READING

Comprehension

1. Why was Dorothy not feeling well when her mother-in-law came to visit?
2. In what way was Dorothy's appearance different from what her mother-in-law expected?
3. How did mother show her approval of Dorothy?
4. What did mother suggest doing with old coffee grounds?
5. What are some of the things that mother considered to be extravagant?
6. How did mother react to the dinner at Mouquin's?
7. How did mother feel about receiving flowers?
8. How much money did mother leave after her death?
9. What did the narrator learn from his mother about money? Was this the lesson she intended to teach him?

Responding to the Story

1. Why does the narrator consider "What do you do with your old coffee grounds?" an unfair question?
2. How is Dorothy different from the narrator's mother? How is he different from his mother?
3. Could the narrator have made his mother happy during either of the visits described? Explain why or why not. If you think he could have made her happy, tell how.
4. Why does the narrator feel that his mother did not know the value of money? Do you agree with him? Explain.
5. Based on the reading, how would you describe the narrator's feelings toward his mother and her feelings toward him?

Vocabulary

Vocabulary Builder

Match each word in the first column with the word or phrase in the second column that is closest to it in meaning.

1. adversity	a. greatly puzzled
2. bewildered	b. pulsing pain
3. confrontation	c. in a way
4. consequence	d. economical
5. contracted	e. pulled together
6. fling (*n.*)	f. result
7. frugal	g. short period of excitement
8. hangover	h. large
9. morsel	i. hard times
10. severe	j. effects of drinking too much alcohol
11. somewhat	k. serious
12. stammered	l. unknowingly
13. substantial	m. small bite
14. throb	n. meeting
15. unwittingly	o. spoke haltingly

Idiom Exercise

Write your own sentence for each of the underlined idioms and phrases.

Example: My attitude about money <u>stems from</u> my mother.
Dorothy's hangover <u>stems from</u> last night's party.

1. Mother was <u>subject to</u> migraine headaches.
2. Mother wanted to say something about the maid, but she <u>held her peace</u>.
3. That day, Dorothy was neither in perfect health nor in <u>high spirits.</u>
4. The activity in the kitchen went into <u>high gear</u> before the dinner party.
5. A good meal <u>struck her as</u> an extravagance.

Word Forms

Fill in the blanks with the correct form of the words listed.

1. confront, confronted, confronting, confrontation
   a. When Dorothy was ____________________ by her mother-in-law's questions, she did not know the answers.
   b. Mother did not want to ____________________ her son about his extravagance.
   c. There was a possibility of a serious ____________________ between the two women.
   d. He always avoided ____________________ his mother about her problems with spending money.
2. sympathized, sympathy, sympathetic, sympathetically
   a. Dorothy's mother-in-law was very ____________________ about her headache.
   b. Her son felt she might have behaved less ____________________ had she known about Dorothy's hangover.
   c. He ____________________ with his mother up to a point.
   d. He couldn't feel much ____________________ when she refused to spend money on even the smallest things.
3. ignored, ignoring, ignorance, ignorant
   a. Because he was angry with her, he ____________________ her completely.
   b. The best way to hide your ____________________ is to keep quiet.
   c. I am totally ____________________ when it comes to choosing a restaurant.
   d. He was ____________________ the problem, hoping it would disappear.

Structure

Review of Irregular Verbs

Some English verbs do not form their past tense by adding *-ed,* which is the regular way.

Exercise 1

Use the correct past tense form of the irregular verb in parentheses.

EXAMPLES: Last night, Dorothy ___*sang*___ (sing) beautifully.

Yesterday, Mother ___*had*___ (have) a severe headache.

1. Last night he __________ (take) his mother out to dinner.
2. We went to many parties, which we knew __________ (strike) Mother as an extravagance.
3. We had __________ (sing) many songs before we left her apartment.
4. Yesterday, she __________ (bring) the coffee grounds to her daughter-in-law's house.
5. Where have you __________ (hide) your money?
6. We __________ (drink) and __________ (sing) all night at the party.
7. "I __________ (know) you were going to mention that," he said to his mother.
8. I have always followed the lesson mother unwittingly __________ (teach) me.
9. Last night, she __________ (fling) the napkin on the floor because she was upset.
10. She __________ (know) I had married an actress.

11. I have ____________________ you some flowers for your birthday.
(buy)

12. Mother ____________________ when she saw the prices on the menu.
(weep)

13. He knew that having a maid ____________________ mother as an
(strike)
extravagance.

14. She ____________________ in a deep sleep after a very exhausting day.
(lie)

15. She ____________________ the packages on the table and then
(lay)
____________________ down to rest.
(lie)

ROLE PLAY: With a classmate, act out the meeting between Dorothy and her mother-in-law. Use as many of the irregular verbs in the above exercise as you can.

Parallelism

In a compound sentence or other sentence where elements are similar, those elements should have a similar grammatical form. This similarity of grammatical form is called **parallelism**. For example, the following is a compound sentence with parallel elements that are grammatically similar:

> My mother was surprised by my wife, and my wife was surprised by my mother.
>
> (my mother   was surprised by my wife, and
> my wife   was surprised by my mother)

Exercise 1

Rewrite the following sentences, correcting for parallelism. In each sentence, where parallel elements of a sentence have different grammatical forms, rephrase the last *element to correct the problem.*

EXAMPLES: The first confrontation had its surprises as well as being difficult.
The first confrontation had its surprises as well as its difficulties.

She bought very little, saved her money, and she lived an unhappy life.
She bought very little, saved her money, and lived an unhappy life.

1. We talked and laughed and were singing all night.
2. Dorothy sat with us at the table, ate little, and she contributed less to the conversation.
3. You could get a good dinner for seventy-five cents, and forty or fifty cents could get you a substantial dinner.

(Continued on next page)

4. While the waiter served the courses and then her untouched plates were removed, mother sat there and was weeping. (Two changes needed—two elements are not parallel.)
5. I thought that she deserved to eat a good dinner and seeing a good show.
6. I can't say that she taught me the value of money, because that she knew the value of money I don't believe.

Exercise 2

Rewrite each of the following sentences according to the suggested pattern. Be sure that you have used parallel structure—that all the verbs are in the same tense and all the elements in the sentence have the same structure.

Example: Dorothy sat with us at the table, ate little, and contributed less to the conversation.
Dorothy was sitting with us at the table, was eating little, and was contributing less to the conversation.

1. They busily set up the screen, adjusted the projector, and arranged the slides for the slide show.
   They were busily ______________________________
   ______________________________.
2. Howard admired his mother for her patience, diligence, and intelligence.
   Howard admired his mother because she ______________________________
   ______________________________.
3. The waiter handed us the menus, took our orders, and brought us our food.
   The waiter's responsibilities included handing us ______________________________
   ______________________________.
4. Howard loved to watch Dorothy while she was singing and dancing.
   Howard loved watching Dorothy ______________________________
   ______________________________.

Exercise 3

Complete the following sentences by filling in the blanks. Use your imagination.

Example: Some good things to eat are fish, ____salad____, and ____bread____.

1 Some good forms of exercise are jogging, ______________________, and ______________________.
2. I enjoy reading books, ______________________, and ______________________.

3. We went to the grocery store and bought flour, ____________________, and ____________________.
4. I want a house that has a large kitchen, ____________________, and ____________________.

Follow Up

Topics for Discussion

1. Mother's attitude toward money affected her ability to enjoy life. Do you think that such an attitude toward money would always affect a person's ability to enjoy life? Why or why not?
2. Although the narrator's mother is clearly an extreme type, most people do make some economies. What are some ways you have learned to save money? What are some of the most interesting ways of economizing that you have seen people come up with? What do you think are some of the most effective ways of economizing? the least effective?
3. One of mother's characteristics is that she is unable to bend—even on special occasions or for very small purchases, she is unable to put aside her idea that spending money is bad. Have you known anyone who was unable to bend or change his or her ideas or behavior? Describe this person, giving your opinion of the reason he or she was this way.
4. The narrator refers to the following lines from William Shakespeare:

   Sweet are the uses of adversity,
   Which, like the toad, ugly and venomous,
   Wears yet a precious jewel in his head . . .

   What are the "sweet" uses of adversity? Do you think that adversity tends to help in these ways or, as the narrator says, to have "horrible and scarifying" effects? Why do different people react differently to adversity?
5. If you could choose, what qualities would you look for in an in-law? What quality would you *least* want to see? What kind of relationship would you want to have? What kind of contribution would you want your in-law to make to your marriage?
6. Mother and son have opposite attitudes toward money. With whom do you agree more? Why? What are some of the advantages of each attitude? some of the dangers of each?

Topics for Writing

1. Write an essay of three or more paragraphs, describing the two philosophies about money and giving reasons why one philosophy is better than the other.
2. Write a letter to a young person in which you give her or him advice about how to deal with money. The letter should make clear your attitude toward money—whether it is like the narrator's or his mother's.
3. In an essay of several paragraphs, describe a stingy person you have known. What were some of the unusual ways in which he or she economized?
4. In an essay of several paragraphs, describe a spendthrift (a person who is careless about money) you have known. In what ways did she or he waste money?
5. With three of your classmates, choose any part of this story and change it into a scene for a play. For example, you might choose mother's first visit to New York, her meeting with Dorothy, or her son's visits to her when she was dying.
6. In three or more paragraphs, write an essay describing how you would live if you had a million dollars.
7. What if the mother in the selection had unexpectedly received a very large sum of money—would she have suddenly changed or would she have remained the same? Write a story in which the mother receives a lot of money.
8. Write a monthly budget, listing what you will spend for things you need and want. Make sure the money you spend is not more than the money you take in.

UNIT 14

The Romance of a Busy Broker

—O. HENRY

About the Author

O. **Henry** *(1862–1910) was the pen name of William Sydney Porter. He wrote extremely popular stories dealing chiefly with the lives of ordinary people in large cities. The stories are marked by sentimentality and often by a surprise ending, which came to be known as the "O. Henry ending" and was widely imitated by other short-story writers. Collections of his stories include* Cabbages and Kings *(1904),* The Four Million *(1906), and* Waifs and Strays *(1917). O. Henry had a contract with the magazine of the* New York Sunday World *to write one story a week, at a rate of $100 per story, and it was a contract he managed to fulfill. In his early career he was a newspaperman and a bank clerk. He served a prison term in Ohio for stealing from the bank, although it is said that the bank's poor bookkeeping methods were responsible for the shortages of funds for which he was blamed.*

Read the following selection, which is taken from The Four Million, *for its overall effect. Don't stop to look up every word, but notice how the author builds up to his surprise ending.*

◆ Previewing the Story

Look at the picture, the title, and the first paragraph of the story. Answer the questions, explaining each answer.

1. What is the profession of the man in the picture? of the woman?
2. Why do you think the man is drawn the way he is?
3. Who might be involved in the romance? What might the romance be like?

◆ Thinking about the Topic

Think about and answer the following questions.

1. What kinds of work do brokers do? What are some of the things they deal with?
2. How can being extremely busy at work affect other areas of a person's life?

Pitcher, confidential clerk* in the office of Harvey Maxwell, broker,[1] allowed a look of mild interest and surprise to visit his usually expressionless countenance[2] when his employer briskly entered at half-past nine in company with his young lady stenographer. With a snappy "Good-morning, Pitcher," Maxwell dashed at his desk as though he were intending to leap over it, and then plunged[3] into the great heap[4] of letters and telegrams waiting there for him.

The young lady had been Maxwell's stenographer for a year. She was beautiful in a way that was decidedly[5] unstenographic. She forewent[6] the pomp[7] of the alluring pompadour.[8] She wore no chains, bracelets, or lockets. She had not the air of being about to accept an invitation to luncheon. Her dress was gray and plain, but it fitted her figure with fidelity[9] and discretion.[10] In her neat black turban hat was the gold-green wing of a macaw.° On this morning she was softly and shyly radiant.[11] Her eyes were dreamily bright, her cheeks genuine peach-blow, her expression a happy one, tinged[12] with reminiscence.[13]

Pitcher, still mildly curious, noticed a difference in her ways this morning. Instead of going straight into the adjoining room, where her desk was, she lingered,[14] slightly irresolute,[15] in the outer office. Once she moved over by Maxwell's desk, near enough for him to be aware of* her presence.

The machine sitting at the desk was no longer a man; it was a busy New York broker moved by buzzing wheels and uncoiling springs.

"Well—what is it?" asked Maxwell, sharply. His opened mail lay like a bank[16] of stage snow* on his crowded desk. His keen[17] gray eye, impersonal and brusque,[18] flashed upon her half impatiently.

"Nothing," answered the stenographer, moving away with a little smile.

[1] one who brings together buyers and sellers
[2] face
[3] dived
[4] pile
[5] definitely
[6] did without
[7] splendid display
[8] woman's fancy hairdo
[9] faithfulness
[10] care; good judgment
[11] glowing
[12] colored
[13] remembrance
[14] stayed on
[15] undecided
[16] pile
[17] sharp
[18] quick

macaw

"Mr. Pitcher," she said to the confidential clerk, "did Mr. Maxwell say anything yesterday about engaging[19] another stenographer?"

"He did," answered Pitcher. "He told me to get another one. I notified the agency yesterday afternoon to send over a few samples this morning. It's 9:45 o'clock, and not a single picture hat or piece of pineapple chewing gum has showed up yet."

"I will do the work as usual, then," said the young lady, "until some one comes to fill the place." And she went to her desk at once and hung the black turban hat with the gold-green macaw wing in its accustomed[20] place.

He who has been denied the spectacle[21] of a busy Manhattan broker during a rush of business is handicapped[22] for the profession of anthropology. The poet sings of the "crowded hour of glorious life." The broker's hour is not only crowded, but minutes and seconds are hanging to all the straps and packing both front and rear platforms.

And this day was Harvey Maxwell's busy day. The ticker[23] began to reel[24] out jerkily[25] its fitful[26] coils of tape, the desk telephone had a chronic[27] attack of buzzing. Men began to throng[28] into the office and call at him over the railing, jovially,[29] sharply, viciously,[30] excitedly. Messenger boys ran in and out with messages and telegrams. The clerks in the office jumped about like sailors during a storm. Even Pitcher's face relaxed into something resembling animation.[31]

On the Exchange* there were hurricanes[32] and landslides and snowstorms and glaciers[33] and volcanoes,[34] and those elemental disturbances were reproduced[35] in miniature in the broker's offices. Maxwell shoved[36] his chair against the wall and transacted business after the manner of a toe dancer. He jumped from ticker to phones, from desk to door with the trained agility[37] of a harlequin.[38]

In the midst of this growing and important stress[39] the broker became suddenly aware of a high-rolled fringe[40] of golden hair under a nodding canopy[41] of velvet and ostrich[42] tips, an imitation sealskin sacque[43] and a string of beads as large as hickory nuts, ending near the floor with a silver heart. There was a self-possessed young lady connected with these accessories,[44] and Pitcher was there to construe[45] her.

"Lady from the Stenographer's Agency to see about the position," said Pitcher.

Maxwell turned half around, with his hands full of papers and ticker tape.

[19] hiring
[20] usual
[21] sight
[22] at a disadvantage; disabled
[23] machine that prints stock market transactions
[24] wind
[25] unevenly
[26] in spurts
[27] long-lasting
[28] crowd
[29] merrily
[30] nastily
[31] liveliness
[32] storms that form over water
[33] huge masses of ice
[34] mountains with openings through which gases, etc., rise from below
[35] copied
[36] pushed
[37] quickness
[38] dancing clown
[39] tension
[40] trimming
[41] overhanging covering
[42] a large bird
[43] short coat
[44] ornamental extras
[45] explain

"What position?" he asked, with a frown.[46]

"Position of stenographer," said Pitcher. "You told me yesterday to call them up and have one sent over this morning."

"You are losing your mind, Pitcher," said Maxwell. "Why should I have given you any such instructions? Miss Leslie has given perfect satisfaction during the year she has been here. The place is hers as long as she chooses to retain[47] it. There's no place open here, madam. Countermand[48] that order with the agency, Pitcher, and don't bring any more of 'em in here."

The silver heart left the office, swinging and banging itself independently against the office furniture as it indignantly[49] departed. Pitcher seized a moment to remark to the bookkeeper that the "old man" seemed to get more absent-minded[50] and forgetful every day of the world.

The rush and pace of business grew fiercer[51] and faster. On the floor* they were pounding[52] half a dozen stocks in which Maxwell's customers were heavy investors. Orders to buy and sell were coming and going as swift[53] as the flight of swallows.[54] Some of his own holdings[55] were imperiled,[56] and the man was working like some high-geared,[57] delicate, strong machine—strung to full tension,[58] going at full speed, accurate, never hesitating, with the proper word and decision and act ready and prompt as clockwork. Stocks[59] and bonds,[60] loans and mortgages,[61] margins[62] and securities[63]—here was a world of finance, and there was no room in it for the human world or the world of nature.

When the luncheon hour drew near* there came a slight lull[64] in the uproar.[65]

Maxwell stood by his desk with his hands full of telegrams and memoranda, with a fountain pen over his right ear and his hair hanging in disorderly[66] strings over his forehead. His window was open, for the beloved janitress,[67] Spring, had turned on a little warmth through the waking registers[68] of the earth.

And through the window came a wandering—perhaps a lost—odor—a delicate, sweet odor of lilac that fixed the broker for a moment immovable. For this odor belonged to Miss Leslie; it was her own, and hers only.

The odor brought her vividly,[69] almost tangibly,[70] before him. The world of finance dwindled[71] suddenly to a speck.[72] And she was in the next room—twenty steps away.

"By George, I'll do it now," said Maxwell, half aloud. "I'll ask her now. I wonder I didn't do it long ago."

[46] displeased look
[47] keep
[48] take back, cancel
[49] angrily
[50] without thought for what one is doing
[51] more violent
[52] knocking down in price
[53] fast
[54] a type of bird
[55] possessions
[56] endangered
[57] high-speed
[58] strain
[59] shares in a company
[60] certificates that promise interest on loaned money
[61] loans made on property
[62] part payments on stocks
[63] stocks and bonds
[64] period of quiet
[65] outburst of noise
[66] messy
[67] cleaning woman
[68] outlets for heating in a room
[69] clearly
[70] able to be touched
[71] became smaller
[72] small spot

He dashed into the inner office with the haste of a short trying to cover.* He charged[73] upon the desk of the stenographer.

[73] came at high speed

She looked up at him with a smile. A soft pink crept over her cheek, and her eyes were kind and frank.[74] Maxwell leaned one elbow on her desk. He still clutched[75] fluttering[76] papers with both hands and the pen was above his ear.

[74] open and honest
[75] held tightly
[76] windblown

"Miss Leslie," he began, hurriedly, "I have but a moment to spare. I want to say something in that moment. Will you be my wife? I haven't had time to make love to you in the ordinary way, but I really do love you. Talk quick, please—those fellows are clubbing the stuffing out of* Union Pacific."[77]

[77] a railroad company

"Oh, what are you talking about?" exclaimed the young lady. She rose to her feet and gazed upon him, round-eyed.

"Don't you understand?" said Maxwell, restively.[78] "I want you to marry me. I love you, Miss Leslie. I wanted to tell you, and I snatched[79] a minute when things had slackened up* a bit. They're calling me for the phone now. Tell 'em to wait a minute, Pitcher. Won't you, Miss Leslie?"

[78] impatiently
[79] grabbed

The stenographer acted very queerly.[80] At first she seemed overcome with amazement;[81] then tears flowed from her wondering eyes; and then she smiled sunnily through them, and one of her arms slid tenderly[82] about the broker's neck.

[80] strangely, oddly
[81] great surprise
[82] lovingly

"I know now," she said, softly. "It's this old business that has driven everything else out of your head for the time. I was frightened at first. Don't you remember, Harvey? We were married last evening at 8 o'clock in the Little Church around the Corner." ◆

Idioms and Phrases*

confidential clerk	*private secretary*
to be aware of	*to sense, to know*
stage snow	*artificial snow as used in the theater*
the Exchange	*New York Stock Exchange*
on the floor	*in the area (of the stock exchange) where business is done*
drew near	*came closer*
a short trying to cover	*stock exchange phrase*
clubbing the stuffing out of	*beating up*
slackened up	*slowed down*

POST-READING

Comprehension

1. How long had Miss Leslie been working for Maxwell?
2. In what city does this story take place? At what time of the year does it take place?
3. Why was Harvey Maxwell so busy? What kinds of business activities were taking place?
4. How did Maxwell treat the woman from the stenographers' agency? Why did he treat her this way?
5. What made Harvey Maxwell think of proposing?
6. What was Miss Leslie's reaction to Mr. Maxwell's proposal?

Responding to the Story

1. What is Miss Leslie like as a person? How does she apparently differ from other stenographers, such as the one who came to be interviewed?
2. What role does Pitcher play in the story? How would the story seem different if Pitcher were not in it?
3. What is Harvey Maxwell like as a person? Do you think it is possible that a man would forget he had been married the night before?
4. Did you find the ending surprising? Looking back at the story, do you see any clues pointing to this ending? Do you like the ending? Why or why not?
5. What kind of marriage do you think Mr. and Mrs. Maxwell will have? Explain your answer.
6. This story takes place around 1900. Do you think it would work if set in today's times? If so, what would have to be changed? If not, why not?

VOCABULARY

Vocabulary Builder

Answer the following questions briefly.

1. Why was Pitcher's *countenance* usually expressionless?
2. Was the stenographer's *adjoining* room near to or far from Mr. Maxwell's office? Is that her *accustomed* place?
3. The stenographer *lingered* slightly *irresolute*. What was she doing? What was she feeling?

(Continued on next page)

4. Is a *keen* look, *impersonal* and *brusque,* a very friendly look? Why or why not?
5. Is a *frank* look an honest look?
6. When you are *engaging* a stenographer, do you give her a diamond ring? If not, what do you give her?
7. Does a *chronic* attack last awhile or is it over quickly?
8. How does Mr. Maxwell's *agility* help him in the course of a busy day?
9. What is the opposite of a *frown*?
10. Would you be worried if your broker told you your investments were *imperiled*? Why or why not?
11. What was the stenographer who *indignantly* departed the office feeling?
12. Do you consider yourself to be an *absent-minded* person? Why or why not?
13. Do you like people who are *prompt*? Why or why not?
14. Is a *lull* in the *uproar* temporary or permanent? Do things *slacken up* a bit?
15. Would you feel comfortable in a *disorderly* office? Why or why not?
16. Is *countermanding* an order a sign of approval?

Adjectives

With each of the underlined words, form adjectives by using the suffix -ous, -y, -ic, -ful, *or* -ing.

EXAMPLES: A look of <u>interest</u>	**An <u>interested</u> look**
A book of <u>interest</u>	**An <u>interesting</u> book**

1. a hairstyle with <u>allure</u>	an ________________ hairstyle
2. a story of <u>romance</u>	a ________________ story
3. a machine with <u>speed</u>	a ________________ machine
4. an employee with a <u>frown</u>	a ________________ employee
5. movements with <u>jerks</u>	________________ movements
6. a man full of <u>pomp</u>	a ________________ man
7. a disturbance like a <u>volcano</u>	a ________________ disturbance
8. a face with a <u>smile</u>	a ________________ face
9. eyes full of <u>wonder</u>	________________ eyes
10. a dash with <u>haste</u>	a ________________ dash

11. an arrival filled with mystery — a ________________ arrival
12. a look of love — a ________________ look
13. an hour of glory — a ________________ hour
14. an ending that surprises — a ________________ ending
15. an absent-mindedness that has danger — a ________________ absent-mindedness
16. a feeling of stress — a ________________ feeling

STRUCTURE

Modifier Patterns

Nouns can be modified with adjectives that precede them or with an adjective following the verb *be*. Structures with *be* may be rewritten in other ways.

Rewrite the sentences using the modifier patterns shown.

1. Pitcher allowed a look of interest and surprise to visit his usually expressionless countenance. —>
   Pitcher allowed an interested and surprised look to visit his usually expressionless countenance.

   a. On uttering the proposal, he saw her eyes fill with a look of wonder and amazement.
   b. There was a young lady of self-possession connected with these accessories.
   c. There was no room in Maxwell's office for the human world or the world of nature.
   d. The sweet odor of lilac caused the broker to stand still.

2. Pitcher was still mildly curious. He noticed a difference in her ways this morning. —>
   Pitcher, still mildly curious, noticed a difference in her ways this morning.

   a. Her dress was gray and plain. It fitted her figure with fidelity and discretion.
   b. The odor of lilac was sweet and delicate. It fixed the broker for a moment immovable.
   c. The accessories were cheap and showy. They were connected with a self-possessed young lady.
   d. The machine was strong and delicate. It worked at full speed without once stopping.

(Continued on next page)

3. He worked like a machine. He was tense, accurate, and unhesitating. —>

   He worked like a machine—tense, accurate, and unhesitating.

   a. She wore appropriate clothes. They were gray and plain but flattering.
   b. On this morning she looked especially beautiful. She looked radiant, dreamy, and happy.
   c. He gave her his usual look. It was impersonal, brusque, and impatient.
   d. Through the window came a wandering odor. It was delicate and sweet and perhaps lost.

Transitional Devices

Transitional devices connect ideas, sentences, and paragraphs. They make writing more unified and clear. Some words used as transitional devices are *afterward, however, then, and, but, as soon as, consequently, another, therefore, at first,* and *as a result.*

Exercise 1

In the paragraph that follows, fill in the appropriate transitional words from the list above. You do not have to use all of the words. You may use any of the words more than once.

On Monday, John bought one hundred shares of common stock. ________________ (1), the price of the stock started to go up. ________________ (2), John wanted to sell the stock when it was two dollars higher than his original cost, ________________ (3) he became greedy, ________________ (4) he decided to hold on to the stock for ________________ (5) few days. He ________________ (6) gave orders to his stockbroker to hold the stock for ________________ (7) month. ________________ (8), John left for his vacation. ________________ (9) he left, the price of the stock began to fall. The broker tried to reach John, ________________ (10) he couldn't. ________________ (11), John lost all his money. ________________ (12) of his experience, John learned not to be greedy.

Exercise 2

Write a paragraph entitled, "My Most Embarrassing Moment." Use as many of these transitional devices as you can: finally, furthermore, still, yet, and, but, then, later, meanwhile, at the same time, for this reason, next.

Conditional: Unreal

An **unreal conditional statement** describes a situation in which the condition is untrue or has not happened. It is expressed by using the simple past tense in the *if* clause and *would, could,* or *might* plus the simple form of the verb in the *result* clause.

Exercise 1

Change the following sentences to unreal conditional statements.

EXAMPLE: If I invest my money wisely, I will make a profit.
If I invested my money wisely, I would make a profit.

1. If Miss Leslie leaves, we will hire another stenographer.
2. If you come late, I won't wait for you.
3. If I see Miss Leslie, I will call you.
4. If it snows, we will close the office.
5. If the ticker breaks, Mr. Maxwell won't know the stock prices.
6. If the stenographer retires, you will get the job.
7. If the weather is nice, I'll walk to the park.
8. If she loves me, I'll propose to her.
9. If the work in the office slows down, I'll go out for lunch.
10. If there is an earthquake, the town will be destroyed.

Exercise 2

Make up ten unreal conditional statements of your own, making sure that you use the simple past tense in the if *clause and* would *plus the simple form of the verb in the* result *clause.*

FOLLOW UP

Topics for Discussion

1. Harvey Maxwell deals in stocks, bonds, mortgages, margins, and securities. If you are familiar with these terms, explain what they mean and what the differences among these things are.
2. What other jobs do you know of that are so busy and pressured? Would you want to work at such a job? If you have worked at such a job, what was it like?
3. Should the human and business worlds be separated, as for Maxwell? What are the advantages and disadvantages of such a separation?

(Continued on next page)

4. The story involves an extremely quick romance—with the proposal and marriage evidently occurring on the same day. In your country what would be normal?
5. In the story, the woman who went for the interview was very extravagantly dressed. How do you think a person should dress for a job interview? for working in an office?
6. Businesses often discourage office romances. What do you think of office romances? Are they a bad idea? Why or why not?

Topics for Writing

1. Mr. Maxwell's proposal is very unusual. Write a story in which you describe a more typical, more romantic proposal.
2. Write a story in which you describe an office romance that takes place in our times.
3. The story suggests some of the advantages and disadvantages of investing in the stock market. If this is something you know about, write an essay of three or more paragraphs, in which you compare the advantages and disadvantages of investing in the stock market with those of keeping your money in the bank.
4. In an essay of three or more paragraphs, describe someone you know or have read about who is as totally involved in his or her business or work as is Mr. Maxwell. How have that individual's personal relationships been affected?
5. Write a letter in which you apply for a job in a brokerage firm. Give a short description of your job history and qualifications.
6. Pretend that you are Miss Leslie, and write a diary entry to cover the two-day period of the story.

UNIT 15

University Days

—JAMES THURBER

About the Author

James Thurber *(1894–1961) is considered the best American humor writer since Mark Twain. He is known for the irony, satire, and whimsical humor of his stories about ordinary American life. He is also known for his masterful cartoons. Thurber lost one eye in a childhood accident, but despite that and the gradual weakening of the other eye over the years, he had a very successful writing career, contributing hundreds of stories, articles, and cartoons to* The New Yorker. *Some of his stories have been made into films, most notably "The Secret Life of Walter Mitty," the film version of which starred Danny Kaye. Thurber's books include* My Life and Hard Times *(1933), from which this story is taken, and* My World and Welcome to It *(1942).*

"University Days" is based on the author's experiences as a student at Ohio State University, which he left in 1918. It is one of the most popular of all his stories. The accompanying drawings are also Thurber's. For ease of reading, we have divided this story into two parts.

◆ Previewing the Story

Look at the picture, the title, and the first paragraphs of Parts I and II of the story. Answer the questions, explaining each answer.

1. What do you think the story is about?
2. What is the state of mind of the older man in the picture? Why do you think the younger man is unhappy?
3. Do you think the two men are friends? Why or why not?
4. Based on the picture and your previewing of the first paragraphs of Parts I and II, what kind of university days do you think the narrator has?

◆ Thinking about the Topic

1. What is the difference between a college and a university?
2. In universities in your country, are there courses students must pass in order to graduate? What are the requirements for graduation?
3. Compare college life in your country with college life in the United States.

PART I

I passed[1] all the other courses that I took at my University, but I could never pass botany. This was because all botany students had to spend several hours a week in a laboratory looking through a microscope at plant cells,[2] and I could never see through a microscope. I never once saw a cell through a microscope. This used to enrage[3] my instructor. He would wander around the laboratory pleased with the progress all the students were making in drawing the involved[4] and, so I am told, interesting structure of flower cells, until he came to me. I would just be standing there. "I can't see anything," I would say. He would begin patiently enough, explaining how anybody can see through a microscope, but he would always end up in a fury,[5] claiming that I could *too* see through a microscope but just pretended that I couldn't. "It takes away from the beauty of flowers anyway," I used to tell him. "We are not concerned with beauty in this course," he would say. "We are concerned solely[6] with what I may call the *mechanics*[7] of flars."[8] "Well," I'd say, "I can't see anything." "Try it just once again," he'd say, and I would put my eye to the microscope and see nothing at all, except now and again a nebulous[9] milky substance—a phenomenon[10] of maladjustment.[11] You were supposed to see a vivid, restless clockwork of sharply defined plant cells. "I see what looks like a lot of milk," I would tell him. This, he claimed, was the result of my not having adjusted[12] the microscope properly, so he would readjust it for me, or rather, for himself. And I would look again and see milk.

I finally took a deferred[13] pass, as they called it, and waited a year and tried again. (You had to pass one of the biological sciences or you couldn't graduate.) The professor had come back from vacation brown as a berry, bright-eyed, and eager to explain cell-structure again to his classes. "Well," he said to me, cheerily, when we met in the first laboratory hour of the semester,[14] "we're going to see cells this time, aren't we?" "Yes, sir," I said. Students to right of me and to left of me and in front of me were seeing cells; what's more,* they were quietly drawing pictures of them in their notebooks. Of course, I didn't see anything.

"We'll try it," the professor said to me, grimly,[15] "with every adjustment of the microscope known to man. As God is my witness, I'll

[1] successfully completed

[2] units of living matter

[3] anger greatly

[4] complicated

[5] rage, extreme anger

[6] only

[7] workings; physical makeup

[8] flowers

[9] cloudlike; indistinct

[10] remarkable or unusual thing; fact

[11] improper correction

[12] corrected

[13] postponed

[14] part of a university year

[15] sternly; with determination

He was beginning to quiver all over, like Lionel Barrymore.

arrange this glass so that you see cells through it or I'll give up* teaching. In twenty-two years of botany, I—" He cut off abruptly for he was beginning to quiver all over, like Lionel Barrymore,[16] and he genuinely wished to hold onto his temper,* his scenes with me had taken a great deal out of him.

So we tried it with every adjustment of the microscope known to man. With only one of them did I see anything but blackness or the familiar lacteal[17] opacity,[18] and that time I saw, to my pleasure and amazement, a variegated[19] constellation[20] of flecks, specks,[21] and dots. These I hastily drew. The instructor, noting my activity, came back from an adjoining[22] desk, a smile on his lips and his eyebrows high in hope. He looked at my cell drawing. "What's that?" he demanded, with a hint[23] of a squeal[24] in his voice. "That's what I saw," I said. "You didn't, you didn't, you didn't!" he screamed, losing control of his temper instantly, and he bent over and squinted[25] into the microscope. His head snapped up. "That's your eye!" he shouted. "You've fixed the lens so that it reflects! You've drawn your eye!"

Another course that I didn't like, but somehow managed to pass, was economics. I went to that class straight from the botany class, which

[16] American stage and movie actor (1878–1954)

[17] milky

[18] not transparent

[19] marked with different colored patches

[20] group of related things

[21] small spots of dirt or color

[22] nearby

[23] slight suggestion or indication

[24] shrill sound indicating pain

[25] looked with half-shut eyes

didn't help me any in understanding either subject. I used to get them mixed up. But not as mixed up as another student in my economics class who came there direct from a physics laboratory. He was a tackle[26] on the football team, named Bolenciecwcz. At that time Ohio State University had one of the best football teams in the country, and Bolenciecwcz was one of its outstanding stars. In order to be eligible[27] to play it was necessary for him to keep up* in his studies, a very difficult matter, for while he was not dumber than an ox, he was not any smarter. Most of his professors were lenient[28] and helped him along. None gave him more hints, in answering questions, or asked him simpler ones than the economics professor, a thin, timid man name Bassum. One day when we were on the subject of transportation and distribution, it came Bolenciecwcz's turn to answer a question. "Name one means of transportation," the professor said to him. No light came into the big tackle's eyes. "Just any means of transportation," said the professor. Bolenciecwcz sat staring at him. "That is," pursued the professor, "any medium, agency, or method of going from one place to another." Bolenciecwcz had the look of a man who is being led into a trap. "You may choose among steam, horse-drawn, or electrically propelled[29] vehicles," said the instructor. "I might suggest the one which we commonly take in making long journeys across land." There was a profound[30] silence in which everybody stirred[31] uneasily, including Bolenciecwcz and Mr. Bassum. Mr. Bassum abruptly broke this silence in an amazing manner. "Choo-choo-choo," he said, in a low voice, and turned instantly scarlet.[32] He glanced appealingly around the room. All of us, of course, shared Mr. Bassum's desire that Bolenciecwcz should stay abreast of* the class in economics, for the Illinois game, one of the hardest and most important of the season, was only a week off. "Toot, toot, too-tooooooot!" some student with a deep voice moaned, and we all looked encouragingly at Bolenciecwcz. Somebody else gave a fine imitation of a locomotive letting off steam. Mr. Bassum himself rounded off* the little show. "Ding, dong, ding, dong," he said, hopefully. Bolenciecwcz was staring at the floor now, trying to think, his great brow furrowed,[33] his huge hands rubbing together, his face red.

"How did you come to college this year, Mr. Bolenciecwcz?" asked the professor. "*Chuf*fa chuffa, *chuf*fa chuffa."

"M'father sent me," said the football player.

[26] a football player in a specific position

[27] qualified, permitted

[28] understanding, easygoing

[29] driven forward

[30] deep

[31] moved slightly

[32] bright red

[33] lined

Bolenciecwcz was trying to think

[34] allowance: an amount of money given to someone regularly

"What on?" asked Bassum.

"I git an 'lowance,"[34] said the tackle, in a low, husky voice, obviously embarrassed.

"No, no," said Bassum. "Name a means of transportation. What did you *ride* here on?"

"Train," said Bolenciecwcz.

"Quite right," said the professor. "Now, Mr. Nugent, will you tell us—" ◆

IDIOMS AND PHRASES*

what's more	*in addition*
give up	*leave, quit*
hold onto his temper	*not become angry*
keep up	*do well enough to continue*
stay abreast of	*keep up with*
rounded off	*finished*

Post-Reading

Comprehension

1. What did the narrator usually see in the microscope instead of flower cells?
2. Why did he take botany over again?
3. When he finally did see something different in the microscope, what was it?
4. How did the botany professor react to the narrator's inability to adjust the microscope properly? Why did the professor lose his temper?
5. What other class besides botany did the author dislike?
6. Why did the author take these two classes even though he didn't like the subjects?
7. What university did the narrator attend?
8. Who was Bolenciecwcz?
9. Why was it important to help him pass his courses?
10. What did a train have to do with economics?
11. How did Bolenciecwcz finally arrive at the right answer?

Responding to the Story

1. Why do you think Bolenciecwcz was accepted into college? Do you think he graduated?
2. How are the narrator's problems in the first anecdote and Bolenciecwcz's problems in the second anecdote similar? How are they different?
3. Do you think the botany professor was right to react as he did to the narrator's problem with the microscope? If not, what would have been a better way to react?
4. Can you sympathize with the narrator's problems? That is, have you ever had similar problems with a course?
5. Do you think the cartoons contribute to the story and its humor? How much of a difference do they seem to make?

VOCABULARY

Vocabulary Builder

Match the words in the first column with the words and phrases in the second column that are closest to them in meaning.

1. adjusted	a. slight suggestion
2. allowance	b. shrill sound
3. deferred	c. looked with half-shut eyes
4. eligible	d. football player
5. furrowed	e. easy
6. grimly	f. driven forward
7. hint	g. moved slightly
8. lenient	h. bright red
9. nebulous	i. amount of money given regularly
10. propelled	j. lined
11. scarlet	k. corrected
12. semester	l. delayed
13. specks	m. indistinct
14. squeal	n. term
15. squinted	o. sternly
16. stirred	p. qualified
17. tackle	q. spots

Idiom Exercise

Exercise 1

Fill in the blanks with the following idioms and phrases. Change the verb forms if necessary.

hold onto his temper
give up
keep up
what's more

1. The narrator would have been happy to ____________________ further study of botany, but the most he could do was to defer it.
2. Even with a lot of help, Bolenciecwcz had an extremely difficult time ____________________ with his economics class.

3. Bolenciecwcz couldn't answer an easy question, and ____________________, he couldn't answer it even when given many hints.
4. That Mr. Bassum was able to ____________________ despite Bolenciecwcz's inability to answer the question was amazing.

Exercise 2

Write a sentence for each of the idioms and phrases listed. Verb forms can be changed.

1. ____
2. ____
3. ____
4. ____

PART II

[1] severe suffering
[2] a place for physical exercise and sports
[3] moving backward and forward
[4] take off one's clothes
[5] tall and lean
[6] questioned closely
[7] school of higher education; a part of a university
[8] reason for saying, doing, or believing something
[9] completely
[10] set
[11] farming
[12] area of responsibility
[13] yet, still

If I went through anguish[1] in botany and economics—for different reasons—gymnasium[2] work was even worse. I don't even like to think about it. They wouldn't let you play games or join in the exercises with your glasses on and I couldn't see with mine off. I bumped into professors, horizontal bars, agricultural students, and swinging[3] iron rings. Not being able to see, I could take it* but I couldn't dish it out.* Also, in order to pass gymnasium (and you had to pass it to graduate) you had to learn to swim if you didn't know how. I didn't like the swimming pool, I didn't like swimming, and I didn't like the swimming instructor, and after all these years I still don't. I never swam but I passed my gym work anyway, by having another student give my gymnasium number (978) and swim across the pool in my place. He was a quiet, amiable blonde youth, number 473, and he would have seen through a microscope for me if we could have got away with it,* but we couldn't get away with it. Another thing I didn't like about gymnasium work was that they made you strip[4] the day you registered. It is impossible for me to be happy when I am stripped and being asked a lot of questions. Still, I did better than a lanky[5] agricultural student who was cross-examined[6] just before I was. They asked each student what college[7] he was in—that is, whether Arts, Engineering, Commerce, or Agriculture. "What college are you in?" the instructor snapped at the youth in front of me. "Ohio State University," he said promptly.

It wasn't that agricultural student but it was another a whole lot* like him who decided to take up* journalism, possibly on the ground[8] that when farming went to hell* he could fall back on* newspaper work. He didn't realize, of course, that that would be very much like falling back full-length[9] on a kit[10] of carpenter's tools. Haskins didn't seem cut out for* journalism, being too embarrassed to talk to anybody and unable to use a typewriter, but the editor of the college paper assigned him to the cow barns, the sheep house, the horse pavilion, and the animal husbandry[11] department generally. This was a genuinely big "beat,"[12] for it took up five times as much ground and got ten times as great a legislative appropriation* as the College of Liberal Arts. The agricultural student knew animals, but nevertheless[13] his stories were dull and colorlessly written. He took all afternoon on each of them, on account of* having to hunt for* each letter on the typewriter. Once in a while* he had to ask somebody to help him hunt. "C" and "L," in particular, were hard letters for him to find. His editor finally got pretty much annoyed at the farmer-journalist because his pieces[14] were so uninteresting. "See here, Haskins," he snapped at him one day, "Why is it we never have anything hot[15] from you on the horse pavilion? Here we have two hundred head of horses on this campus—more than any other university in the Western Conference[16] except Purdue[17]—and yet you never get any real low down* on them. Now shoot over* to the horse barns and dig up* something lively." Haskins shambled out and came back in about an hour; he said he had something. "Well, start it off snappily,"[18] said the editor. "Something people will read." Haskins set to work and in a couple of hours brought a sheet of typewritten paper to the desk; it was a two-hundred word story about some disease that had broken out among the horses. Its opening sentence was simple but arresting.[19] It read: "Who has noticed the sores[20] on the tops of the horses in the animal husbandry building?"

Ohio State was a land grant* university and therefore two years of military drill* was compulsory.[21] We drilled with old Springfield rifles and studied the tactics of the Civil War even though the World War was going on at the time. At 11 o'clock each morning thousands of freshmen[22] and sophomores[23] used to deploy[24] over the campus, moodily creeping up on the old chemistry building. It was good training for the kind of warfare that was waged[25] at Shiloh[26] but it had no connection with what was going on in Europe. Some people used to think there was German money behind it, but they didn't dare[27] say so or they would have been thrown in jail as German spies. It was a period of muddy[28] thought and marked, I believe, the decline of higher education in the Middle West.

As a soldier I was never any good at all. Most of the cadets[29] were glumly[30] indifferent[31] soldiers, but I was no good at all. Once General Littlefield, who was commandant of the cadet corps, popped up* in front of me during regimental drill and snapped, "You are the main trouble with the university!" I think he meant that my type was the main trouble with the university but he may have meant me individually. I was mediocre[32] at drill certainly—that is, until my senior year. By that time I had drilled longer than anybody else in the Western Conference, having

[14] writings
[15] new; impressive
[16] a group of colleges that play sports with each other
[17] a university in Indiana
[18] in a lively manner
[19] attention-catching
[20] painful spots
[21] something that must be done
[22] first-year students
[23] second-year students
[24] spread out in line of battle
[25] carried on
[26] Civil War battleground
[27] have the courage to
[28] unclear
[29] students taking military training
[30] sadly
[31] uncaring
[32] not very good, second-rate

[33] been unsuccessful
[34] the one before
[35] connecting cities
[36] an actor
[37] someone employed by a hotel to carry luggage
[38] confidence
[39] thorough
[40] military movements (British spelling)
[41] do

failed[33] at military at the end of each preceding[34] year so that I had to do it all over again. I was the only senior still in uniform. The uniform which, when new, had me look like an interurban[35] railway conductor, now that it had become faded and too tight made me look like Bert Williams[36] in his bellboy[37] act. This had a definitely bad effect on my morale.[38] Even so, I had become by sheer[39] practice little short of wonderful at squad manoeuvres.[40]

One day General Littlefield picked our company out of the whole regiment and tried to get it mixed up by putting it through one movement after another as fast as we could execute[41] them: squads right, squads left, squads on right into line, squads right about, squads left front into line, etc. In about three minutes one hundred and nine men were marching in one direction and I was marching away from them at an angle of forty degrees, all alone. "Company halt!" shouted General Littlefield. "That man is the only man who has it right!" I was made a corporal for my achievement.

[42] called
[43] hitting with a sharp blow
[44] back
[45] caused to move or jump
[46] distant

The next day General Littlefield summoned[42] me to his office. He was swatting[43] flies when I went in. I was silent and he was silent too, for a long time. I don't think he remembered me or why he had sent for me, but he didn't want to admit it. He swatted some more flies, keeping his eyes on them narrowly before he let go* with the swatter. "Button up your coat!" he snapped. Looking back on it now I can see that he meant me although he was looking at a fly, but I just stood there. Another fly came to rest on a paper in front of the general and began rubbing its hind[44] legs together. The general lifted the swatter cautiously. I moved restlessly and the fly flew away. "You startled[45] him!" barked General Littlefield, looking at me severely. I said I was sorry. "That won't help the situation!" snapped the General, with cold military logic. I didn't see what I could do except offer to chase some more flies toward his desk, but I didn't say anything. He stared out the window at the faraway[46] figures of co-eds crossing the campus toward the library. Finally, he told me I could go. So I went. He either didn't know which cadet I was or else he forgot what he wanted to see me about. It may have been that he wished to apologize for having called me the main trouble with the university; or maybe he had decided to compliment me on my brilliant drilling of the day before and then at the last minute decided not to. I don't know. I don't think about it much any more. ◆

Idioms and Phrases*

(to) take it	*(to) bear trouble*
dish it out	*treat someone roughly*
got away with it	*did it without being caught or punished*
a whole lot	*very much*
take up	*begin to do, or learn*
went to hell	*became ruined*
fall back on	*turn to, rely on*
cut out for	*suited for*
legislative appropriation	*money given by the government for a specific purpose*
on account of	*because of*
hunt for	*look for*
once in a while	*occasionally*
low down	*inside facts*
shoot over	*hurry*
dig up	*find; get*
land grant	*public land given by the government*
military drill	*army training*
popped up	*appeared suddenly*
let go	*attacked*

Post-Reading

Comprehension

1. For what reasons did the narrator dislike gymnasium?
2. How did the narrator pass his swimming test?
3. Why couldn't the narrator pass botany the same way?
4. Does the narrator think highly of the agriculture students at the college? How can you tell?
5. Why was Haskins unsuited for journalism?

Responding to the Story

1. What do you think are the narrator's strengths and weaknesses as a student?
2. In your opinion, why is this story humorous? What does it make fun of?
3. Do you think that anything about the narrator's attitude toward his school emerges from these anecdotes? If so, what?

Vocabulary

Vocabulary Builder

Exercise 1

In your own words, define the following words.

1. gymnasium
2. maneuvers
3. bellboy
4. cadets
5. morale

Exercise 2

Match the words in the first column with their antonyms in the second column.

1. startled	a. front
2. hind	b. following
3. preceding	c. contentment
4. mediocre	d. still
5. muddy	e. stocky, stout
6. compulsory	f. dress
7. lanky	g. voluntary
8. strip	h. clear
9. swinging	i. first-rate
10. anguish	j. unsurprised

Idiom Exercise

Fill in the blanks with the idiom or phrase that means the same thing as the words in parentheses. Put verbs into the correct form.

a whole lot	low down
cut out	on account of
dig up	once in a while
dish it out	pop up
fall back on	shoot over
get away with it	take it
hunt for	take up

1. He can ______________________, but not very graciously.
   (bear unpleasantness)
2. His idea was ______________________ journalism at the university.
   (to learn)

3. Journalism would give him something to ____________________ (turn to) if farming didn't work out.

4. Don't ____________________ (treat roughly) unless you can stand criticism in return.

5. He thought he could ____________________ (do it without being caught), but his nervousness gave him away.

6. He had just about given up with the microscope when a pattern of specks, flecks, and dots ____________________ (appeared suddenly).

7. It's unlikely that he ever felt like ____________________ (hurrying over) to gym, botany, economics, or military drill.

8. The editor wanted the ____________________ (facts) on the horses in the barn.

9. He was good at drill ____________________ (because of) having had several years of practice.

10. ____________________ (Occasionally), Bolenciecwcz managed to answer an economics question.

11. Some people are not ____________________ (suited) for agriculture.

12. His problems with gym were ____________________ (very much) like his problems with botany but easier to resolve.

13. Asked to ____________________ (find) an exciting angle on horses, Haskins ____________________ (looked for) one all over but without much success.

Word Forms

Fill in the correct form of the words listed.

1. explain, explained, explaining, explanation
   a. He would begin by ____________________ that anybody could pass botany if he or she could see through a microscope.
   b. His ____________________ of transportation and distribution was very complicated.
   c. Please ____________________ why you are so late for class.
   d. Bolenciecwcz ____________________ that he was very serious about passing economics.

(Continued on next page)

2. adjust, adjusted, adjusting, adjustment
   a. ____________________ the microscope in order to see plant cells was very difficult for the botany student.
   b. The professor made a small ____________________ on the microscope, but I could only see a milky substance.
   c. He quickly ____________________ to university life.
   d. When you live with others in the same house, you must learn to ____________________ your schedule to theirs.
3. demand, demanded, demanding
   a. There is a great ____________________ for good football players.
   b. Mr. Bassum, the economics professor, was very lenient and not ____________________.
   c. He ____________________ that I show him my homework.
   d. He was ____________________ that we all write articles for the school newspaper.
4. arrange, arranged, arranging, arrangements
   a. If you don't do your homework, I will ____________________ to hire a tutor for you.
   b. I made ____________________ for another student to take my swimming test.
   c. He ____________________ for Haskins to write the article.
   d. ____________________ the schedule took all his energy.

Courses of Study and Professions

Fill in the second column with the profession that matches the course of study listed in the first column.

Example: If you study *botany*, you will become a *botanist*.

If you study	you will become a
1. law	____________________
2. journalism	____________________
3. accounting	____________________
4. biology	____________________
5. chemistry	____________________
6. economics	____________________
7. psychology	____________________
8. art	____________________
9. music	____________________

10. geology ____________________
11. engineering ____________________
12. physics ____________________
13. architecture ____________________
14. philosophy ____________________
15. history ____________________
16. mathematics ____________________
17. medicine ____________________

STRUCTURE

Transition Words: Coordinating Conjunctions, Subordinating Conjunctions, and Conjunctive Adverbs

Clauses in a sentence can be joined by several types of words—coordinating conjunctions, subordinating conjunctions, and conjunctive adverbs.

The **coordinating conjunctions** are *and, but, for, so, yet, or,* and *nor.* They can be used to connect two independent clauses, that is, two clauses that are themselves grammatically complete sentences. For example, the clauses in the following sentence are separated by a comma.

He hated gym, and he didn't much care for botany.

Subordinating conjunctions begin a subordinate clause—a clause that, because of the subordinating conjunction, cannot stand alone. Subordinating conjunctions include *after, although, because, before, if, since, unless, until, while,* and many others. These conjunctions link the subordinate clause to the independent clause. When the subordinate clause is first, the clauses are separated by a comma. In the following example, the subordinate clause is first, but it can occur in either position.

Though he didn't much care for botany, he found gym far worse.

Conjunctive adverbs are adverbs that connect two independent clauses. Clauses connected with conjunctive adverbs are separated by a semicolon, rather than by a comma. The conjunctive adverb can occur at various places in the second clause and is set off from the rest of the clause in which it occurs by a

(Continued on next page)

comma. The following is an example of clauses connected with a conjunctive adverb:

He didn't much care for botany; however, he found gym far worse.

In contrast to coordinating and subordinating conjunctions, **conjunctive adverbs** can also tie together the ideas in separate sentences. The preceding example could be restated as,

He didn't much care for botany. However, he found gym far worse.

OR

He didn't much care for botany. Gym, however, he found far worse.

There are many conjunctive adverbs, including *accordingly, also, certainly, consequently, finally, furthermore, however, in addition, in fact, instead, moreover, nevertheless, then, therefore,* and *thus.*

Exercise 1

Fill in the blanks with the correct coordinating conjunction, subordinating conjunction, or conjunctive adverb.

EXAMPLE: He screamed, losing control of his temper instantly, ___*and*___ (also/and) he bent over and squinted into the microscope.

1. He would begin patiently enough, explaining how anybody can see through a microscope, ____________ (but/however) he would always end up in a fury.
2. He claimed this was the result of my not having adjusted the microscope properly, ____________ (so/therefore) he would readjust it for me.
3. Students to the right of me and to the left of me and in front of me were seeing cells; ____________ (and/furthermore), they were quietly drawing pictures of them in their notebooks.
4. He cut off abruptly, ____________ (for/so) he was beginning to quiver all over, ____________ (and/in addition) he genuinely wished to hold onto his temper.

5. The instructor noted my activity, ____________________ he came
(and/but)
back with his eyebrows high in hope.

6. ____________________ Bolenciecwcz was not dumber than an ox, he
(Whereas/Wherever)
was not any smarter.

7. All of us, of course, shared Mr. Bassum's desire that Bolenciecwcz should stay abreast of the class in economics, ____________________
(consequently/for)
the Illinois game was only a week away.

8. This was a genuinely big "beat," ____________________ it took up
(for/yet)
five times as much ground and got ten times as great a legislative appropriation as the College of Liberal Arts.

9. The agricultural student knew animals; ____________________, his
(moreover/nevertheless)
stories were dull and colorlessly written.

10. Here we have two hundred head of horses on this campus,

____________________ you never get any real low down on them.
(however/yet)

11. Ohio State was a land grant university; ____________________, two
(so/therefore)
years of military drill was compulsory.

12. We studied the tactics of the Civil War ____________________ the
(as though/even though)
World War was going on at the time.

13. It was good training for the kind of warfare that was waged at Shiloh,

____________________ it had no connection with what was going on in
(but/however)
Europe.

14. Some people used to think there was German money behind it,

____________________ they didn't dare say so ____________________
(but/however) (nor/or)
they would have been thrown in jail.

Exercise 2

Use the words in the list to combine sentences in rewriting the paragraph. Use all the words, and use each word only once. (There is more than one way of rewriting the paragraph.)

although	however
and	in addition
finally	so
first of all	therefore

Example: I passed all the other courses that I took at my university. I could never pass botany.
I passed all the other courses that I took at my university, but I could never pass botany.

He hated botany. He found gym worse, for several reasons. They wouldn't let students play games with their glasses on. He couldn't see with his off. Knowing how to swim was a requirement. He didn't know how to swim! He had to learn. Another student agreed to take the test for him. He was able to fulfill the requirement.

Punctuation: Commas and Semicolons

Punctuate the following sentences by inserting commas and semicolons. In some items, the need for punctuation is related to the distinctions discussed in the text about conjunctions; some items involve other rules of punctuation, most of which have been covered in earlier chapters.

Example: Ohio State was a land grant university therefore two years of military drill was compulsory.
Ohio State was a land grant university; therefore, two years of military drill was compulsory.

1. Haskins shambled out and came back in about an hour he said he had something.
2. "Well start it off snappily" said the editor. "Something people will read."
3. Haskins brought a sheet of typewritten paper to the desk it was a two-hundred word study about some disease that had broken out among the horses.
4. Haskins wanted to take up journalism he didn't realize however that that would be very much like falling back full-length on a kit of carpenter's tools.
5. Most of the cadets were glumly indifferent soldiers but I was no good at all.
6. Once General Littlefield who was commandant of the cadet corps popped up in front of me during regimental drill and shouted "You are the main trouble with this university!"

7. Even so I had become by sheer practice little short of wonderful at squad maneuvers.
8. He swatted flies keeping his eyes on them narrowly before he let go with the swatter.
9. Finally he told me I could go.
10. You were supposed to see a vivid restless clockwork of sharply defined plant cells.

Conditional: Past Unreal

In a past statement in which the condition is unreal or untrue, we use the past perfect tense in the *if* clause and *would have, could have,* or *might have* plus the past participle in the result clause.

EXAMPLES: If they *had let* (let) him wear glasses, he *would have won* (win) some games.

If I *had not gone* (not go) to class, I *would not have met* (not meet) Bolenciecwcz.

Change the following sentences to past unreal conditional statements. Make sure you use the correct form of the verb in parentheses.

1. If the agricultural student __________ (know) how to type well, he __________ (write) his stories faster.
2. If Haskins __________ (dig) up something lively, he __________ (get) it published.
3. Thurber __________ (enjoy) university life if he __________ (not have) to participate in military drill.
4. If he __________ (not fail) at military, he __________ (not take) it again the following year.
5. If General Littlefield __________ (not forget) why he had sent for me, he __________ (praise) my military skill.
6. If Bolenciecwcz __________ (not maintain) his class standing, he __________ (have) to leave the university.
7. If he __________ (be) able to swim, he __________ (pass) the test.

Follow Up

Topics for Discussion

1. Describe some amusing events that have happened to you or around you in school.
2. What courses do you dislike the most in school, and why?
3. Do you believe that some people actually have learning blocks in certain subjects—in mathematics or foreign languages, for example? Why do you or don't you believe this? Defend your opinion with specific examples.
4. Are there any specific courses or procedures that you would like to see changed in your school? Is there anything that seems particularly silly or unreasonable? Explain fully.
5. The issue of college sports and student athletes has become a major one. Critics charge that schools often recruit athletes who lack academic skills and then don't teach them those skills. They feel that sports should be given less emphasis and that all students should meet the schools' requirements fully. Are you familiar with this issue? What do you think?

Topics for Writing

1. In an essay of three or more paragraphs, compare the advantages and disadvantages of a university education with the advantages and disadvantages of studying for a trade.
2. In an essay of three or more paragraphs, write about what subjects you excel in and what profession you would like to pursue.
3. Write about a teacher or professor whom you liked or disliked and tell why.
4. Write a shorter "University Days" or "School Days" story of your own. Like Thurber's story, your story should include details about courses, professors and students, and events at a particular school you attended.
5. Write a newspaper story, giving "the real low down" on some topic related to your current school. Follow the advice of the college newspaper editor in "University Days": "Start it off snappily" and make sure it's "something people will read." Include a headline.

Answer Key

Unit 1

Vocabulary

Vocabulary Builder

1. register
2. nature
3. transact
4. resort to
5. state, desolately
6. perspiration
7. blasphemy
8. reminiscence
9. nastier
10. readjustment

Idiom Exercise

EXERCISE 1

1. I beg your pardon
2. It's like this

Word Forms

1. a. connection
   b. connect
   c. connecting
2. a. transact
   b. transaction
   c. transacting
3. a. wrapping, wrap
   b. Wrap
   c. wrapper

Structure

Verb Tenses

1. has, will go
2. went
3. has or had
4. takes
5. speaking, realized
6. spoke
7. left
8. thought
9. feel
10. call, need
11. gave
12. give
13. will give
14. bought, will buy

Say and *Tell*

1. told	5. said
2. said, tell	6. said
3. told	7. told
4. told	8. said

Direct and Indirect Speech

EXERCISE 1

1. Mr. Seeley told the operator that his wife had bought some flour three days ago.
2. The store employee told Mr. Seeley that she would connect him with the grocery department.
3. The grocery department employee asked Mr. Seeley if he wished to register a complaint.
4. The employee asked Mr. Seeley for his address.
5. Mr. Seeley told the employee that he had just given her his address.
6. Mr. Seeley said desolately that he had worms.
7. The readjustment department employee asked Mr. Seeley to tell him what readjustment he wished.
8. Mr. Seeley answered that he wanted to be sent some flour without worms.

Sentence Builder: Various Idioms

EXERCISE 1

1. a. I beg your pardon. We didn't mean to send the wrong package.
   b. I beg your pardon. I didn't mean to hurt your feelings.
   c. I beg your pardon. I didn't mean to take your credit card.
2. a. I want to tell you about my complaint.
   b. I want to tell you about my meeting with the store manager.
   c. I want to tell you about my problem with the complaint department.
3. a. They could hardly wait to see their friends again.
   b. We could hardly wait for the delivery of our new computer.
   c. I can hardly wait to see how the new coat I bought for Tom fits him.

Adverbs with *Say* and *Tell;* Other Speech Verbs

1. shouted
2. desolately
3. wearily
4. politely
5. confidently
6. asked
7. answered
8. firmly
9. insisted
10. angrily
11. threatened

Unit 2

Vocabulary

Vocabulary Builder

1. h
2. g
3. i
4. j
5. a
6. c
7. b
8. d
9. f
10. e

Word Forms

1. a. arrival
   b. arrived
   c. arriving
2. a. eventful
   b. event
   c. uneventfully
3. a. detain
   b. detained
   c. detention
4. a. delighted
   b. delightful
   c. delight
5. a. appreciate
   b. appreciative
   c. appreciation

Structure

Articles

1. an
2. a
3. the
4. the
5. the
6. a
7. the
8. the
9. a

Verb Tenses

1. has changed
2. happens
3. met
4. spent
5. have met
6. lifted
7. got, studied
8. study
9. will not/won't move
10. Get, fail

Sentence Builder: Imperatives and Polite Requests

1. a. May I see it?
   b. Tell me what you did in school.
   c. Try to do better on the next test.
   d. Explain this poor grade to me.
   e. Tell me what a leaf looks like.
2. a. Won't you trust me, Dad?
   b. Could you move your hand?
   c. Could you turn off the TV?
   d. Could you do your homework with the TV off?
   e. Could you show me your homework?

Unit 3

Vocabulary

Vocabulary Builder

1. seriously
2. went to bed
3. lateness
4. bad habits and qualities
5. cleaning/repair people
6. university administrator
7. business administrator
8. on purpose
9. fellow worker
10. strolled
11. rather large
12. possibility
13. good qualities
14. took on
15. important
16. shiny
17. accident
18. quick
19. calmly
20. came together

Structure

Pronouns

Exercise 1

1. his, his, it, his, his
2. They, their, their
3. They, nobody
4. him, them
5. he, him
6. His, her, she, it, she
7. his
8. his, her
9. another, he
10. his, who
11. he, himself
12. they, their
13. his, he
14. him, them, their
15. it

Active and Passive Voice

1. His secretary gave him the impression that the engagement was for twelve-thirty.
2. Actually, the secretary set the engagement for one o'clock.
3. George reserved the honeymoon suite.
4. The garage attendant washed George's car before the wedding.
5. His father warned her of his lateness.
6. His father promoted George in no time.
7. His father also gave George an increase.
8. When the old man died, George assumed the presidency of the plant.
9. George often told the story of his late arrival.
10. The driver and his assistant replaced the flat tire.

Articles

1. Ø
2. the, the
3. Ø, a, the, the
4. the, the, an, the
5. the
6. the
7. The, the
8. an
9. an, Ø
10. a, a
11. The
12. a, a
13. a
14. a
15. a
16. the, the
17. the
18. The, Ø, the

Prepositions

Exercise 1

1. with
2. about
3. of
4. to
5. on
6. on
7. in
8. after
9. for
10. of
11. into
12. of
13. into
14. to
15. with
16. over
17. around
18. for
19. In
20. in

Past Perfect Tense

1. was, had done
2. had wiped, announced
3. arrived, had folded
4. received, had ended
5. made, had finished
6. was, had instructed
7. became, had received
8. had become, continued
9. told, had stopped
10. had detected, gave

Unit 4

Vocabulary

Vocabulary Builder

1. awful
2. self-evident
3. grave
4. irresponsible
5. threshold
6. fetched
7. crumpled
8. presume
9. gathered
10. convulsive
11. ghastly
12. intend
13. wretched
14. astonished
15. thrust
16. reckless

Idiom Exercise

Exercise 1

1. led the way
2. swam before his eyes
3. too far gone
4. led the way
5. swam before his eyes
6. too far gone

Word Forms

1. a. responsible
   b. responsibilities
   c. irresponsible
2. a. doubtful
   b. doubt
   c. doubted
3. a. imply
   b. implication
   c. implied
4. a. Swimming
   b. swimmer
   c. swam
5. a. intentions
   b. intended
   c. intending
6. a. impressive
   b. impressed
   c. impression
7. a. interruption
   b. interrupting
   c. interrupt

Structure

Spelling

Exercise 1

a. staring
b. presuming
c. rising
d. snapping
e. proposing
f. sitting
g. attempting
h. writing
i. swimming
j. crumpling
k. plunging

Exercise 2

a. salaries
b. lives
c. miseries
d. keys
e. agencies
f. echoes
g. fifties
h. mysteries
i. sixes
j. businesses
k. gentlemen

It's and *Its*

Exercise 1

1. it's
2. It's
3. its
4. it's
5. it's
6. it's, its, its
7. its
8. its
9. It's, its

Combining Sentences with *And*

Exercise 1

1. I crossed the threshold of a bank, and I attempted to transact business.
2. My salary had been raised to fifty dollars a month, and I felt that the bank was the only place for it.
3. I shambled in and looked timidly at the clerks.
4. We both sat down and looked at each other.
5. I knew what he was thinking, and it made me feel worse.
6. I propose to deposit fifty-six dollars now and fifty dollars a month regularly.
7. The manager got up and opened the door.
8. He made me write the sum on a slip and sign my name in a book.
9. Someone gave me a checkbook through a window, and someone else began telling me how to write it out.
10. I hoped that they might think something had insulted me while I was writing the check and I had changed my mind.
11. I keep my money in cash in my trousers pocket and my savings in silver dollars in a sock.

Subject-Verb Agreement

1. tries
2. want
3. were
4. has
5. has
6. feels
7. has
8. keep
9. have
10. wish

Regular and Irregular Past Tense Verbs

1. I knew this, but I felt the bank was the only place for it.
2. I held my fifty-six dollars clutched in a crumpled ball.
3. He felt that I had an awful secret to reveal.
4. He led the way to a private room and turned the key in the lock.
5. "Good morning," I said, and stepped into the safe.
6. I wrote something on the check and thrust it in at the clerk.
7. As the big door swung behind me, I caught the echo of a roar of laughter that went up to the ceiling of the bank.
8. I banked no more, but kept my money in my trousers pocket.

Cloze Exercise

1. rattle
2. cross
3. awful
4. swims
5. and
6. ghastly
7. forge
8. It's
9. transact
10. to make
11. withdraw
12. seems
13. misery
14. going

Unit 5

Vocabulary

Vocabulary Builder

1. a
2. d
3. c
4. a
5. d
6. c
7. d
8. a

Idiom Exercise

Exercise 1

1. c
2. b
3. c

Structure

Adjectives and Adverbs

1. good
2. well
3. carefully
4. careful
5. intentionally
6. natural
7. intentional
8. attractive
9. amiable
10. pleasantly
11. particularly
12. beautifully

Sentences with *Let's*

Exercise 1

1. Let's not speak of the matter again.
2. Let's not give it another thought.
3. Let's sit down and let's not look around.
4. Let's go in and eat.
5. If she speaks, let's pretend to be deaf.

Combining Sentences by Using Relative Pronouns

1. The tall man who is wearing a blue shirt looks like an impostor.
2. Melik saw the young lady who was sitting in the diner.
3. Melik offered another young man a cigarette, which he accepted.
4. The trip which we discussed yesterday was finally approved.
5. The man who was in a hurry ran to the train.
6. Some strangers who look very safe are dangerous.
7. The travelers, who were holding hands, were running down the street.
8. Melik and his friend, who were carrying suitcases, walked to the station.
9. Tip the porter who carries your luggage generously.
10. The seat, which is near the window, belongs to the young lady.

Quotation Marks

EXERCISE 1

"Let's not speak of the matter again," the old man said. "It's finished. I have seven children. My life has been a full and righteous one. Let's not give it another thought. I have land, vines, trees, cattle, and money. One cannot have everything—except for a day or two at a time."

"Yes, sir," my uncle said.

"On your way back to your seat from the diner," the old man said, "you will pass through the smoker. There you will find a game of cards in progress. The players will be three middle-aged men with expensive-looking rings on their fingers. They will nod at you pleasantly and one of them will invite you to join the game. Tell them, 'No speak English.' "

"Yes, sir," my uncle said.

"That is all," the old man said.

"Thank you very much," my uncle said.

"One thing more," the old man said. "When you go to bed at night, take your money out of your pocket and put it in your shoe. Put your shoe under your pillow, keep your head on the pillow all night, and don't sleep."

UNIT 6

Vocabulary

Vocabulary Builder

EXERCISE 1

1. i	3. d	5. e	7. h	9. a
2. b	4. c	6. j	8. f	10. g

EXERCISE 2

1. boundless	6. smart
2. sarcastic	7. drawn by
3. spontaneous	8. considerate
4. trivial	9. jovially
5. dreads	10. makes every effort

Word Forms

1. a. dreading
   b. dreadful
   c. dread
2. a. spontaneity
   b. spontaneous
   c. spontaneously
3. a. performed
   b. performance
   c. performing
4. a. considering
   b. considerate
   c. consider
   d. consideration

Structure

Present Perfect and Past Perfect Tenses

EXERCISE 1

1. had (never) put, has (never) gotten
2. had read
3. has tried
4. had (just) started
5. had received
6. hadn't paid
7. haven't pleased
8. has been, have been
9. has been, had (ever) been

It's and Its

1. it's	5. its	9. It's
2. its	6. its	10. It's, it's
3. it's	7. it's, its	
4. it's	8. its	

Appositives

1. Maggie, my wife, was at the kitchen sink.
2. I'd just started reading the paper when Sammy, our five-year-old, came in.
3. His watch, a Christmas present, wasn't wound.
4. Roy, his older brother, told him that he needed to wind it.

Sentence Combining

1. Before I wrote my list, I read books on self-improvement.
2. Maggie, my wife, was at the sink when I came downstairs.
3. I'd started reading the paper when Sammy, our five-year-old son, came in.
4. He was wearing a watch that he had received for Christmas.
5. In order to establish some kind of rapport, I struck up a conversation with Kit.

UNIT 7

Vocabulary

Vocabulary Builder

EXERCISE 1

1. yes	3. no	5. yes
2. yes	4. yes	6. no

EXERCISE 2

1. yes	4. no	7. no	10. no
2. yes	5. no	8. yes	11. yes
3. yes	6. yes	9. yes	

People and Languages

2. Chinese, Chinese
3. Frenchman or Frenchwoman, French
4. Iraqi, Iraqi or Arabic
5. Swede, Swedish
6. Norwegian, Norwegian
7. Dane, Danish
8. Greek, Greek
9. Nepalese, Nepalese
10. German, German
11. Russian, Russian
12. Japanese, Japanese
13. Italian, Italian
14. Irishman or Irishwoman, Irish or Gaelic
15. Turk, Turkish
16. Pole, Polish
17. Mexican, Spanish
18. Israeli, Hebrew
19. Dutchman or Dutchwoman, Dutch

Structure

Who and *Whom*

1. who	5. who	9. whom
2. Who	6. who	10. whom
3. Whom	7. who	11. who
4. whom	8. who.	

Comparatives
1. A trout in the hand is better than a salmon in the pool.
2. To have a thing in your hand is better than waiting for two things.
3. Two birds in the bush are worse than a bird in the hand.
4. Tempers in Scandinavia are cooler than tempers in France.
5. The woman at the Spanish embassy was friendlier than the woman at the French embassy.
6. The narrator received less help from the Turkish embassy than from the Nepalese embassy.
7. The response from the Turkish embassy was more puzzling than the responses from the other embassies.
8. It was noisier in the Italian embassy than in the other embassies.
9. The response from the Soviet embassy took longer than the responses from the other embassies.

Unit 8

Vocabulary

Vocabulary Builder
1. erect
2. temples
3. silly
4. treat
5. fooling, annoyed
6. stretch
7. nasty
8. overwhelming
9. ease
10. collapse
11. care

Idiom Exercise

Exercise 1

1. true	3. false
2. true	4. false

Word Forms

1. a. easing	c. ease
b. easily	d. easy
2. a. comforting	c. comfortable
b. comfort	d. comforted
3. a. insistence	c. insist
b. insistent	d. insisting
4. a. amusement	c. amused
b. amusingly	d. amusing

Structure

Punctuation
1. The maître d'hôtel was a little worried because Peter wouldn't stop singing, but he really didn't mind.
2. People, when they drink too much whiskey, do foolish things.
3. "Just send her some flowers, and she'll be all right," he said.
4. Peter, a character in the story, seems very confused.
5. Peter is a character in this story. He seems very confused.
6. The girl described his drinking, singing, laughing, and falling.
7. In the morning, I thought I had lost my head; however, I found it under the bed.
8. The song he sang made everyone laugh, even though no one understood it.
9. "Look at me," he said. "My hands are trembling."

Unit 9

Vocabulary

Idiom Exercise
1. bore a resemblance
2. be in touch
3. had reservations about
4. get hold of
5. make up
6. backed up

Word Forms
1. a. frustrate
   b. frustration
   c. frustrating
2. a. irrelevant
   b. relevant
   c. relevance
3. a. disparagingly
   b. disparaging
   c. disparage
   d. disparagement
4. a. apprehension
   b. apprehensively
   c. apprehensive

Structure

Would (Future in the Past) and *Will* (Future in the Present)

1. would	4. would	6. will
2. will	5. would	7. will
3. would		

Past Perfect and Future Perfect Tenses

Exercise 1
1. had already begun
2. had already decided
3. had taken
4. had become
5. had learned

Real and Unreal Conditionals

Exercise 1
1. were, would
2. had, would
3. rented, would
4. is, will
5. wants, will
6. went out, would
7. had, would
8. grooms, will

Infinitives and Gerunds

Exercise 1
1. to spend
2. to be
3. to design
4. attempting to fly
5. predicting
6. to play
7. to walk
8. to arrange to teach
9. vibrating
10. calling, warning

Unit 10

Vocabulary

Vocabulary Builder

1. c	4. b	7. d	10. a	13. c
2. c	5. a	8. a	11. b	14. a
3. c	6. b	9. c	12. a	15. d

Structure

Possessives
1. Mr. Jones's hat
2. Melpomenus's death
3. one month's board
4. two months' board
5. the family's children
6. the children's bedroom
7. the angels' call

Modals

Exercise 1

1. can't	4. need not	7. needn't
2. can	5. should	8. might
3. must	6. couldn't	9. could

Past Continuous Tense

EXERCISE 1

1. was drinking, thought
2. was ending, was falling, looked
3. came, sat
4. was looking
5. left, was playing
6. was meaning
7. was
8. walked, was looking
9. died
10. said, were calling

UNIT 11

Vocabulary

Advise and *Advice*

1. advised	5. advise	9. advice
2. advise	6. advice	10. advises
3. advice	7. advice	
4. advice	8. advised	

Structure

Infinitives and Gerunds

1. to find
2. buying
3. trying on
4. to knock
5. to encourage
6. to purchase
7. selling, to lose
8. closing
9. to make
10. firing
11. to be
12. to discourage
13. to get
14. to risk, insulting
15. to sell
16. taking

Relative Clauses

1. Many young people have a tendency to be too honest, which can play havoc in the retail business.
2. These are just expensive clothes, which women use to compensate for feeling insecure.
3. You have an inner beauty that you try to disguise.
4. She is buying that suit to get back at her husband, whom she suspects of infidelity.
5. The second customer, who was motivated by insecurity, didn't need an evening dress.
6. The store owner fired Miss Brampton, who discouraged customers from making purchases.
7. Miss Brampton, who is a psychology major, is not an effective saleswoman.
8. The owner, whose dress shop is in Georgetown, has had trouble with saleswomen.

Sentence Builder: Constructions with *It*

A.1. It is hard to find hotpants that fit well.
2. It is easy to find expensive evening dresses.
3. It is hard to compensate for insecurities.

B.1. It was inevitable that Miss Brampton would be fired.
2. It was clear that Miss Brampton was not an effective salesperson.
3. It was obvious to everyone but Miss Brampton that the customer was displeased.

What Clauses for Emphasis

EXERCISE 1

1. What she suspected him of was infidelity.
2. What she wanted was to get even.
3. What I advise you to do is think it over for a few days.
4. What the customer felt was considerable anger.
5. What the lady wanted was something really exciting.
6. What she wanted was to go to the Kennedy Center and impress everyone.
7. What people really care about is your inner beauty.
8. What the shop owner wants now is a business major.

UNIT 12

Vocabulary

Vocabulary Builder

1. c	4. a	7. c	10. a	13. a
2. d	5. a	8. a	11. b	14. a
3. a	6. c	9. a	12. d	15. a
				16. c

Word Forms

1. a. intrusion c. intruded
   b. intruding d. intruder, intrusion
2. a. flattery c. flattered
   b. flattering d. flatterer
3. a. absorbing c. absorb
   b. absorption d. absorbed
4. a. contemplating
   b. contemplative
   c. contemplated
   d. contemplation

Structure

Conjunctions: *And* versus *But*

EXERCISE 1

1. and	4. but	7. but	9. and
2. but	5. and	8. but	10. but
3. but	6. and		

Complex Sentences

1. Dan and the ship's surgeon and I had been up to the great square and were on our way to the theatre when we met the General, the Judge, the Commodore, the Colonel, and the Commissioner, who told us to buy some kid gloves.
2. At the same time that I paid the bill, I thought I detected a gently ironical light in the woman's eye, and she was laughing all to herself about something or other.

UNIT 13

Vocabulary

Vocabulary Builder

1. i	4. f	7. d	10. k	13. h
2. a	5. e	8. j	11. c	14. b
3. n	6. g	9. m	12. o	15. l

Word Forms

1. a. confronted
   b. confront
   c. confrontation
   d. confronting
2. a. sympathetic
   b. sympathetically
   c. sympathized
   d. sympathy
3. a. ignored
   b. ignorance
   c. ignorant
   d. ignoring

Structure

Review of Irregular Verbs

EXERCISE 1

1. took	9. flung
2. struck	10. knew
3. sung	11. bought
4. brought	12. wept
5. hidden	13. struck
6. drank, sang	14. lay
7. knew	15. laid, lay
8. taught	

Parallelism

EXERCISE 1

1. We talked and laughed and sang all night.
2. Dorothy sat with us at the table, ate little, and contributed less to the conversation.
3. You could get a good dinner for seventy-five cents, and a substantial dinner for forty or fifty cents.
4. While the waiter served the courses and then removed her untouched plates, mother sat there and wept.
5. I thought that she deserved to eat a good dinner and see a good show.
6. I can't say that she taught me the value of money, because I don't believe she knew its value.

EXERCISE 2

1. They were busily setting up the screen, adjusting the projector, and sitting down to watch the movie.
2. Howard admired his mother because she was patient, diligent, and intelligent.
3. The waiter's responsibilities included handing us the menus, taking our orders, and bringing us our food.
4. Howard loved watching Dorothy sing and dance.

UNIT 14

Vocabulary

Adjectives

1. alluring	6. pompous	11. mysterious
2. romantic	7. volcanic	12. loving
3. speedy	8. smiling	13. glorious
4. frowning	9. wondering	14. surprising
5. jerky	10. hasty	15. dangerous
		16. stressful

Structure

Modifier Patterns

1. a. On uttering the proposal, he saw her eyes fill with a wondering and amazed look.
   b. There was a self-possessed young lady connected with these accessories.
   c. There was no room in Maxwell's office for the human or natural world.
   d. The sweet lilac odor caused the broker to stand still.
2. a. Her dress, gray and plain, fitted her figure with fidelity and discretion.
   b. The odor of lilac, sweet and delicate, fixed the broker for a moment immovable.
   c. The accessories, cheap and showy, were connected with a self-possessed young lady.
   d. The machine, strong and delicate, worked at full speed without once stopping.
3. a. She wore appropriate clothes—gray and plain, but flattering.
   b. On this morning she looked especially beautiful—radiant, dreamy, and happy.
   c. He gave her his usual look—impersonal, brusque, and impatient.
   d. Through the window came a wandering odor—delicate, sweet, and perhaps lost.

Transitional Devices

EXERCISE 1

On Monday, John bought one hundred shares of common stock. Afterward, the price of the stock started to go up. Consequently, John wanted to sell the stock when it was two dollars higher than his original cost, but he became greedy, and he decided to hold on to the stock for another few days. He therefore gave orders to his stockbroker to hold the stock for another month. Then, John left for his vacation. As soon as he left, the price of the stock began to fall. The broker tried to reach John, but he couldn't. Consequently, John lost all his money. As a result of his experience, John learned not to be greedy.

Conditional: Unreal

EXERCISE 1

1. If Miss Leslie left, we would hire another stenographer.
2. If you came late, I wouldn't wait for you.
3. If I saw Miss Leslie, I would call you.
4. If it snowed, we would close the office.
5. If the ticker broke, Mr. Maxwell wouldn't know the stock prices.
6. If the stenographer retired, you would get the job.
7. If the weather was (were) nice, I would walk to the park.
8. If she loved me, I would propose to her.
9. If the work in the office slowed down, I would go out for lunch.
10. If there was (were) an earthquake, the town would be destroyed.

UNIT 15

PART I

Vocabulary

Vocabulary Builder

1. k	5. j	9. m	12. n	15. c
2. i	6. o	10. f	13. q	16. g
3. l	7. a	11. h	14. b	17. d
4. p	8. e			

Idiom Exercise

EXERCISE 1

1. give up
2. keeping up
3. what's more
4. hold onto his temper

PART II

Vocabulary

Vocabulary Builder

EXERCISE 2

1. j	3. b	5. h	7. e	9. d
2. a	4. i	6. g	8. f	10. c

Idiom Exercise

1. take it
2. to take up
3. fall back on
4. dish it out
5. get away with it
6. popped up
7. shooting over
8. low down
9. on account of
10. once in a while
11. cut out
12. a whole lot
13. dig up, hunted for

Word Forms

1. a. explaining c. explain
   b. explanation d. explained
2. a. Adjusting c. adjusted
   b. adjusted d. adjust
3. a. demand c. demanded
   b. demanding d. demanding
4. a. arrange c. arranged
   b. arrangements d. Arranging

Courses of Study and Professions

1. lawyer
2. journalist
3. accountant
4. biologist
5. chemist
6. economist
7. psychologist
8. artist
9. musician
10. geologist
11. engineer
12. physicist
13. architect
14. philosopher
15. historian
16. mathematician
17. doctor or physician

Structure

Transition Words: Coordinating Conjunctions, Subordinating Conjunctions, and Conjunctive Adverbs

EXERCISE 1

1. but
2. so
3. furthermore
4. for, and
5. and
6. Whereas
7. for
8. yet
9. nevertheless
10. yet
11. therefore
12. as though
13. but
14. but, or

EXERCISE 2

<u>Although</u> he hated botany, he found gym worse, for several reasons. <u>First of all,</u> they wouldn't let students play games with their glasses on, <u>and</u> he couldn't see with his off. <u>In addition,</u> knowing how to swim was a requirement; <u>however,</u> he didn't know how to swim! <u>Therefore,</u> he had to learn. <u>Finally,</u> another student agreed to take the test for him, <u>so</u> he was able to fulfill the requirement.

Punctuation: Commas and Semicolons

1. Haskins shambled out and came back in about an hour; he said he had something.
2. "Well, start it off snappily," said the editor. "Something people will read."
3. Haskins brought a sheet of typewritten paper to the desk; it was a two-hundred word study about some disease that had broken out among the horses.
4. Haskins wanted to take up journalism; he didn't realize, however, that that would be very much like falling back full-length on a kit of carpenter's tools.
5. Most of the cadets were glumly indifferent soldiers, but I was no good at all.
6. Once General Littlefield, who was commandant of the cadet corps, popped up in front of me during regimental drill and shouted, "You are the main trouble with this university!"
7. Even so, I had become, by sheer practice, little short of wonderful at squad manoeuvres.
8. He swatted flies, keeping his eyes on them narrowly before he let go with the swatter.
9. Finally, he told me I could go.
10. You were supposed to see a vivid, restless clockwork of sharply defined plant cells.

Conditional: Past Unreal

1. had known, would have written
2. had dug, would have gotten
3. would have enjoyed, had not had
4. had not failed, would not have taken
5. had not forgotten, would have praised
6. had not maintained, would have had
7. had been, would have passed

Copyrights and Acknowledgments

For permission to use the selections reprinted in this book, the authors are grateful to the following publishers and copyright holders:

THE BODLEY HEAD, London For "My Financial Career" and for "The Awful Fate of Melpomenus Jones" by Stephen Leacock, both from *Literary Lapses (The Bodley Head Leacock).* Reprinted by permission of the publisher.

ART BUCHWALD For "The Soft Sell" from *I Never Danced at the White House* (1971), by Art Buchwald. Reprinted by courtesy of the author.

DODD, MEAD & COMPANY For "My Financial Career" from *Laugh with Leacock* by Stephen Leacock. Copyright 1930 by Dodd, Mead & Company, Inc., copyright renewed 1958 by George Leacock. Also for "The Awful Fate of Melpomenus Jones" from *Stephen Leacock's Laugh Parade.* Copyright 1940 by Dodd, Mead & Company, Inc., copyright renewed 1968 by Stephen L. Leacock. Both reprinted by permission of Dodd, Mead & Company, Inc.

GERALD DUCKWORTH & CO. LTD., London For "You Were Perfectly Fine" by Dorothy Parker from *The Collected Dorothy Parker* (Duckworth, 1973). Reprinted by permission of the publisher.

HAMISH HAMILTON LTD., London For "University Days," text and illustrations by James Thurber, from *Vintage Thurber.* The Collection Copyright ©1963 Hamish Hamilton Ltd., London. Reprinted by permission of the publisher.

HARCOURT BRACE JOVANOVICH, INC. For "Old Country Advice to the American Traveler" by William Saroyan. Copyright 1939, 1967 by William Saroyan. Text and illustration reprinted from his volume *My Name Is Aram* by permission of Harcourt Brace Jovanovich, Inc.

MARTIN LEVIN For "A Bird in Hand—What's It Worth?" by Elaine Hart Messmer and for "What Do You Do with Your Old Coffee Grounds?" by Howard Lindsay, both from *The Bedside Phoenix Nest,* edited by Martin Levin. Copyright © 1965 by Martin Levin. Reprinted by permission.

J. B. LIPPINCOTT COMPANY For "Harpist on Horseback" from *Quiet, Yelled Mrs. Rabbit* by Hilda Cole Espy. Copyright ©1958 by J. B. Lippincott Company. Reprinted by permission of Harper Collins Publishers.

LAURENCE POLLINGER LIMITED, London For "Old Country Advice to the American Traveler" from *My Name Is Aram* by William Saroyan. Reprinted by permission of the publisher.

WILL STANTON For "This Year It's Going to be Different" from *The Reader's Digest Bedside Reader—An Anthology of 101 Great Stories* (1970). Reprinted by permission of the author.

HELEN THURBER For "University Days," text and illustrations by James Thurber, from *My Life and Hard Times.* Published by Harper & Row, New York. Copyright ©1933, 1961 James Thurber. Originally printed in *The New Yorker.*

THE VIKING PRESS, INC. For You Were Perfectly Fine" by Dorothy Parker from *The Portable Dorothy Parker.* Copyright 1929, ©1957 by Dorothy Parker. Reprinted by permission of The Viking Press. Originally appeared in *The New Yorker.*

WILLIAM MORRIS AGENCY, INC. For "Are You Majoring in Detention?" by Bill Cosby from *Childhood.* Reprinted by permission of the William Morris Agency, Inc. on behalf of the Author. Copyright ©1991 by William H. Cosby, Jr.

WOOD/FREEMEN For "The Late Mr. Adams" from *Fourteen for Tonight* by Steve Allen (1955). Reprinted by permission.